I love everyone,
well, not as much as I
love my sons Nico + Noel

Love you, MOM
LuLu

the 1000 most asked questions about

ask

the 1000 most asked questions about
love

Jenny Hare

spruce

A Hachette Livre UK Company

First published in Great Britain in 2009 by Spruce,
a division of Octopus Publishing Group Ltd.
2–4 Heron Quays, London E14 4JP
www.octopusbooks.co.uk
www.octopusbooksusa.com

Distributed in the United States and Canada
by Hachette Book Group USA
237 Park Avenue
New York NY 10017

ISBN 13 978-1-84601-293-8
ISBN 10 1-84601-293-7

CIP catalogue record of this book is available from the British Library.

Printed and bound in China

10 9 8 7 6 5 4 3 2 1

Contents

Introduction 6

What is love?
    The meaning & aspects of love 8

The importance of loving yourself
    & each other 46

Looking for love & falling in love 90

Getting on together 134

Communication 182

Lasting love 222

Trust 266

Sex & wellbeing 304

Life stages 340

Fading love 388

Index 428

Introduction

Love is so simple, isn't it? We meet, we're attracted,
get to know and like each other and think we'll always
be together. Love just happens, surely? As an agony
aunt and relationship counsellor for many years, I've
realized that love doesn't stand a chance unless its
looked after with tender, loving care and perseverance.
Love often is spontaneous, of course. But it's rarely as
simple as that all through a relationship; in fact is it
ever? For love, the kind that lasts and is true, is a deep
emotion, and it needs caring for with all your heart,
mind and soul if it's to live up to its full potential.

So is love hard work? Approached lovingly and
willingly, no! But it does, often, take conscious thought
and, always, lots of ongoing energy, commitment and
enthusiasm. Looking after love can become a habit
we hardly notice; natural and, yes, spontaneous. But

we need to provide the right environment and that means not neglecting each other, or the relationship, but being aware of how you both are and taking an interest in each other's thoughts, feelings and interests. It means looking at any difficulties or questions as they arise and considering the best way to resolve them so both of you are content and feel respected and valued.

Even so, when I was asked to write this book I thought, *Goodness, one thousand questions about love in relationships? There can't be that many!* How wrong I was. The questions and answers flowed steadily, and I've addressed the issues that come up most for couples and everyone looking for love too. It's a good idea to prepare for love, because there's so much to learn that will encourage love to live and thrive.

Love is the most important dimension in our lives generally and in any happy relationship. Live with love in your heart and your hands and it will light up your life.

I wish you solutions. I wish you love.

Jenny Hare

What is love?

The meaning & aspects of love

"What does love feel like?"

Love feels like a recognition of all that is good, a delightful warmth in your heart, abundant generosity and tenderness.

"What does love mean?"

Love means many things. Principally, love is kind, patient, humble and does not envy.

"Are there different aspects to love?"

Yes. We can love someone in many ways, including romantically, affectionately and as a close friend.

"Should we try to be everything to each other?"

No, for if you enjoy yourselves when you're on your own you'll have all the more to share with each other when you're together.

"Love isn't always a positive, happy state, is it?"

Love gives us sorrows and joys, puzzles and wonders, but the joys and wonders surpass all else.

"Is it juvenile to say our love is the most important thing in the world to us?"

No. It's wonderful to hear. Carry your love proudly, for it is this world's greatest treasure.

"It's said that we're more likely to be happy if we're in a good relationship. Why is this?"

A relationship involves caring for, and being cared for by, your loved one. Together with the romantic and sexual connection it's a fantastic combination.

"Is a loving relationship the happiest way of life?"

It's certainly a great place to be, but many single people are happy and contented.

"Is true love unconditional?"

Yes, in that you love each other's true self. But negligence or abuse can destroy even the deepest love.

"Do you think that a relationship is a living thing?"

Yes. It's a living thing that needs us to care for it and that, in return, cares for us.

"Does love involve self-sacrifice?"

Love often means putting the other person first and being selfless in our care, but martyrdom has no place in love.

"Can it be true that my partner bullies me because, he says, he loves me?"

No. Love has no part in bullying or aggression. Seek help and get away from him until and unless he has therapy for his problems and has reformed.

"Is a marriage that's been torn apart and then mended more fragile?"

No, for the repair can draw you closer, deepen your understanding and create an even stronger union than before.

"There's plenty of love in my life. Do I really need a loving relationship too?"

Not necessarily, but love with a partner is a wonderful way to be at home with love.

"Is it good to be like my aunt who, although not oblivious to my uncle's faults, always finds something good to say about him?"

Yes. Looking for the silver lining is an excellent way to rationalize differences and remember the love you share.

"As our love deepens, will we lose the magic of being in love?"

Not if you see it as the launching point for an even more beautiful and fulfilled love.

"Our possessiveness makes us both anxious. How can we relax and enjoy our love without behaving as if we own each other?"

Talk about the difference between possessiveness and love and, as you release the strings you've tied, then your love will shine with joy and so will you.

"What are the greatest gifts we can give each other?"

Mutual respect and kindness. They cost nothing and are love's greatest treasures.

"What's the point of love?"

Many people believe that love in general is the whole point of our existence. And love with a partner feels fantastic!

"If love were a picture, what would it look like?"

Enjoy imagining your own picture of what love means to you; it will be different for everyone.

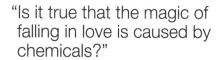

"Is it true that the magic of falling in love is caused by chemicals?"

In a way, yes, because the in-love feelings are caused by chemicals that make us feel good and give us a high.

"What causes attraction?"

A complex mix of psychological and physical factors, including pheromones that appeal emotionally and strike a chord in our brains.

"It's as though loving my partner has lit up my whole life. I feel happier and fitter, and I'm full of energy. Can love cause these physical and mental changes?"

Yes. Loving and being loved release a chain of physical and psychological reactions that make us feel healthier and more positive.

"Is sexual desire good for me?"

If the feeling is pleasant and doesn't harm anyone, yes.

"Why does desire feel good even if my partner doesn't want to make love?"

It gives a satisfying feeling of being in touch with your sexuality.

"Does a climax have a lasting effect?"

In the immediate aftermath, endorphins give a wonderful feeling of wellbeing, and if you recall this memory throughout the day it can make you feel good all over again.

"Are there extra benefits to having orgasms regularly?"

Yes, because they're easier and often stronger if you enjoy them often.

"Is mutual sexual satisfaction beneficial for a relationship?"

Yes, definitely. It gives a great feeling of intimacy and a rush of love for each other.

"Can I affect my own wellbeing and our relationship by thinking loving thoughts of my partner?"

Yes. If we think lovingly, love grows and irritations fade or are resolved.

"Is love good for our health?"

Yes, extremely. Physically, feeling loving releases feel-good hormones like endorphins. Psychologically, it can be exhilarating or relaxing. Either way, it's uplifting.

"Is arousal good for us in health terms?"

Yes. The increased blood flow helps keeps tissues healthy.

"Is it true that having an orgasm is good for you?"

Yes. It makes you feel good and has many health benefits, including improved blood flow and a long-lasting feeling of wellbeing.

"Are rows and resentments between us bad for our health?"

Yes. Sharp words or careless actions cause hurt, sap the energy of both of you and make it difficult to feel loving or loved.

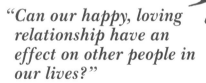

"Can our happy, loving relationship have an effect on other people in our lives?"

Yes. Love surrounds you with an aura that, perhaps unbeknown to those around you, will lift their spirits.

"There are things that I've never told anyone that I'd like to tell my partner. Should I?"

Yes. Love enables you to share each other's sorrows as well as joys, and it will deepen when you do.

"Our shared eccentricity makes us feel very close friends. But should we try to squash our eccentricity and be more normal?"

Continue to be your natural selves. Quirkiness was something you each fell in love with, and long may it last because your relationship will never be boring!

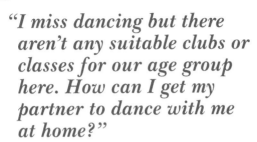

"I miss dancing but there aren't any suitable clubs or classes for our age group here. How can I get my partner to dance with me at home?"

Let him choose the music, and when you start dancing he'll join you.

"When we were first together we always had music on. Would it help us bring back that loving feeling?"

Yes. Listening to good music together is companionable and is food for the soul and for love.

"Apart from dancing, is there a sport that would make us feel close and maybe even sensuous too?"

Yes, swimming makes us feel supple and attractive, and it's easy and companionable to go swimming together.

"Is it important for a relationship to cultivate fun?"

Shared fun and laughter make you feel intimate and good together, and they can be a great aphrodisiac. A definite yes!

"We're not great talkers. Is there another easy way to enjoy some mental interaction at home each day?"

Brainteasers of any sort: crossword puzzles, sudoku, tangrams. They'll make you think, laugh and, provided that you don't get competitive, you'll feel as if you're working as a team.

"We have different tastes in television and books. Apart from making love, what else can we do in the winter evenings together?"

Games aren't just for children. Stimulating games like Scrabble or cards are just as much fun for couples.

"Do we need to do things together in our leisure time?"

Yes, doing things together gives you opportunities for sharing pleasure, fun, challenges and peak experiences. You could take up a new hobby together or try joining in with each other's existing interests.

"Our marriage is getting boring. Should I lever my husband off the sofa away from the television?"

Yes! Variety is the spice of love. Revitalize your friendship by sharing other interests and activities that appeal to you both.

"Is it reasonable to want us to go out and about and have a good social life together?"

Yes. It's a great way to enjoy and develop the loving bond between you.

"Is romance sexual?"

Yes, romance is about the mystery of love,
sex and sensuality. It's a seam of gold
running through a relationship.

"Is romance more important to some people than a complete sexual relationship?"

Yes. People who fear or abstain from sex for
another reason often find that romance is a
great alternative form of lovemaking.

"When we were initially in love I always wanted sex but now I rarely do. Can I re-create that feeling?"

Yes. Remember how you used to feel and let the
sensations flood over you.

"Illness has put an end to sex, but can I try to keep an element of romance?"

Yes. Romance will continue to light up your love. Enjoy!

"We've agreed to be celibate, as it's what we both want, but can we still enjoy our sexuality?"

Very much so. Awareness of it will warm you both, and your relationship, whether or not you have sex.

"Only responsibilities keep us together, but is it ok to still enjoy sex even though it's hardly lovemaking?"

Yes, if it doesn't cause emotional hurt. But why not do it with a loving attitude and perhaps your love will grow again.

"How can I be aroused when I'm so tired every evening after work?"

Think of it as a way to relax and ease your tiredness. Take time to get close and begin to make love, and arousal will arrive along with the energy for it.

"I'm not in such good shape as I used to be. How can my partner possibly fancy me?"

Because she finds the whole you sexy, including your body; that's love.

"I'm no gymnast in bed. Does lovemaking need to be athletic?"

No. You and your partner can have a wonderfully sensuous time quietly and peacefully.

"As a couple who have met and fallen for each other late in life, would lovemaking enhance our relationship?"

Yes. As an expression of love, good sex complements intimacy and gives an amazing sense of unity.

"Is it ok for one partner to be passive and rely on the other to take the lead?"

If you're both happy with this dynamic, it's fine.

"What does it take to be good in bed?"

It's about taking an interest in and advocating your partner's and your own pleasure.

"Is it necessary to dress erotically to excite your partner?"

It can be fun. The important thing to remember is that, whatever you're wearing, taking it off can be erotic.

"How can we create an erotic oasis in our tiny flat?"

Love is the same in the most modest or palatial home: heaven on earth.

"My partner doesn't like wearing scent and I miss it. Should I insist he does?"

Respect his preference, but you can enjoy the scent you'd choose for him by using it on yourself or perfuming the room with it.

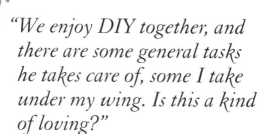

"We enjoy DIY together, and there are some general tasks he takes care of, some I take under my wing. Is this a kind of loving?"

Practical teamwork is a great way to show and enjoy your love for each other.

"Is it unfriendly of me to want my own room now we live together?"

It's natural to need a room or other space in your home that you think of as your own, especially when you're accustomed to it.

"We both believe in women's equality, so although we both work, why do I still do the lion's share of the housework and shopping?"

Because you do it. It's time to stop! The loving way is to divide the household chores fairly between you.

"Odd working hours mean we can't share the chores equally, so how do we avoid feeling the other's shirking?"

Agree that whoever gets home first does the housework, and you'll be pleased at how smoothly and fairly everything gets done.

"The housework exhausts my wife, so how can I persuade her to let me help with what she sees as her responsibility?"

Point out good leadership is about delegating.

"How can I let my partner help me with domestic jobs when he doesn't have a clue?"

Step back and he'll soon learn.

"Will my partner's new passion for a hobby mean he'll love me less?"

No, because it's a different kind of love.

"Will having different religions adversely affect our love?"

Not as long as you are tolerant and respectful of each other's beliefs.

"How can we stop fighting about our opposing religious views?"

By recognizing that the existence of a higher power can't be proved or disproved and agreeing to respect each other's opinions.

"Neither of us believes in God, so how can there be a spiritual side to our love?"

When you feel the wonder of this amazing world the love that flows through it will resonate with the love between you.

"Sometimes our lovemaking's so special it feels like a different dimension. Does anyone else feel like this?"

Yes. The intimacy and joy of love and making love can feel blissfully spiritual.

"My partner's directionless. How can I help her find herself?"

Love accepts that she is on her own path and will find herself and search for the meaning of life in her own time, in her own way.

"Is our belief in a higher power, although we've different faiths, relevant to our relationship?"

Yes. It's good because you can empathize about your core belief of the greater goodness.

"Although we're not sure about religion, we both feel strongly that we'd like to get married in church. Why is this?"

Love is enabling you to listen to heaven's music with your hearts.

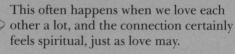

"Is it wrong to marry in church when we're not believers?"

No. God or the greater goodness will rejoice at your presence and commitment to love.

"Does the way we often connect intuitively mean we share some kind of spiritual link?"

This often happens when we love each other a lot, and the connection certainly feels spiritual, just as love may.

"Will our growing sense of our spirituality enhance our marriage?"

Yes, for it will add another precious element to the intimacy you share.

"We find it difficult to express our sense of a spiritual dimension. Should we try?"

There is no need to talk about it unless you feel inspired to. Often simply holding hands or giving each other a hug communicates more fluently an understanding shared.

"Would a commitment enhance our love?"

Yes, if you both want to give it.

"How could living together and/or marrying improve our relationship?"

It tends to give a definite sense of durability and permanence that makes you feel secure and frees you to explore and develop your love.

"My fiancé says we're soul mates. I'm delighted, but what does he mean?"

You connect in all love's ways: as friends, as lovers, spiritually and mentally.

"Intimacy attracts but scares me at the same time. Will I lose my sense of self?"

No. Intimacy is the space you each reach out and fill between your two unique identities.

"Do we need to be compatible in all possible areas of our relationship?"

Friendship alone can sustain a relationship. Usually, though, it helps to be in tune sexually, spiritually and practically, too.

"Can we be soul mates and independent beings?"

Yes. The two complement each other beautifully.

"Is it whimsical to feel our love is helping us grow as people?"

No, it's very real. Love does help us evolve.

"We feel we're part of each other, but will we lose our identity?"

No. The wonderful connection you experience will allow you to respect and cherish your individuality, for that's what you love about each other.

"I can't imagine life without him; I would miss him so much. Is this love?"

Yes, it is. Enjoy it, enjoy each other.

"If we're very intimate, does our love need to be demonstrative?"

Yes, because occasionally one of you may secretly feel unsure of the other's love. So reach out and touch each other's heart with words of love or another romantic gesture.

"After several years of marriage can we become soul mates this late in our relationship?"

Yes. It's mostly about taking an interest in each other in all the aspects of your lives and life together.

"We get on so much better now we've been together a while. Does maturity make love easier?"

Yes. Love, like our personalities, ripens as we mature.

"Our relationship isn't the one I dreamed about, but I realized the other day I'm very content. Is that enough?"

Yes. Love can't be based on expectations. Contentment is love on a firm foundation.

"It's as if we've been lovers before in past lives. Could this be possible?"

No one knows for sure, but couples who love each other deeply often have this sense.

"Why do we seem to have been helped by our differences and disputes over the years whereas some of our friends' marriages have fallen apart?"

Every long-term relationship sees some stumbles and falls, but it's couples who, like you, pick themselves up and recover that last the course.

"Our life and lives together have woven a marriage of beauty and strength. Can we sit back and enjoy it now?"

Enjoy it to the full, but keep weaving the story of your love forever.

"When we met we both felt as if we'd come home. Is this what love is all about?"

Yes. Where two hearts meet is home.

The importance of

loving yourself & each other

"Can you love your partner if you don't love yourself?"

Yes, but you'll enjoy your love, and their love for you, far more if you have the confidence and self-esteem made possible by liking and loving yourself.

"To avoid putting too much pressure on my partner, how can I be less needy emotionally?"

By building and maintaining good friendships and by thinking of yourself as your own best friend.

"Should I have the confidence to say no sometimes?"

Yes. It's important to make your own decisions and stick by them. Your partner will respect you for this.

"My life and our relationship have become very dull. Is this par for the course?"

Goodness no. You should expect and go for a lot, lot more. Start by cherishing your partner with a passion and let the energy flow into every area of your life.

"I'm very shy and find it hard to let anyone get close to me, but I want to be close to my new partner. How can I summon the courage to let him get to know the real me?"

Love inspires confidence and will give you the courage to show your real self to your partner. There's no need to rush; gradually and gently he will get to know you just as you get to know him.

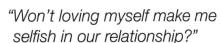

"Won't loving myself make me selfish in our relationship?"

On the contrary, loving yourself will stop you being over-dependent or demanding of your partner.

"Will how I think of myself affect our relationship?"

Yes, because thinking well of yourself will encourage others to do so as well, including your partner.

"If I like myself, will I treat my partner better?"

Yes, because compassion, kindness and love for others start within.

"Isn't it narcissistic to like myself?"

No! Besides, if you are loving and kind to yourself you'll be much nicer to your partner.

"How can I be the kind of person my boyfriend wants to settle down with?"

Don't even try. The surest way to gain confidence is to do your best at being you and to rejoice in your own uniqueness.

"Will it help our relationship if we're both self-confident?"

Hugely, because then you'll automatically deal confidently with issues as they arise.

"If I stifle my feelings will it help our relationship?"

No, only if you recognize, respect and take care of your feelings will your partner be able to do the same.

"How can I have the confidence to say what I mean to my partner?"

Confidence will come more and more easily as you engage in speaking your truth, and it will give honesty to your relationship too.

"My partner would love me to be less timid socially, but how can I override this natural tendency?"

Make a conscious effort to act confidently and with self-assurance and you will find that you soon will be.

"Our relationship suffers from my negativity. How can I be more positive?"

By thinking of your positive thoughts as sensible and useful and your negative thoughts as non-helpful and not worth entertaining.

"Is there an affirmation I can make to hold my own with my partner who has a very strong character?"

Yes, remind yourself: I have tremendous innate personal power to stand up for myself. You'll glow with quiet confidence.

"Neither of us is good at solving any problem in our relationship; we go round and round in circles, worrying. What should we do?"

Instead of obsessing about details, relax and wait for the most sensible way forward to appear; it will.

"Surely my partner and I need to be practical and realize that we do have negative issues sometimes?"

Every couple does, but address them in the confidence that you can deal effectively with them.

"He says he'd love me to be successful like him, but I'm happy how I am and I'm not ambitious, so how can I match up to his aspiration?"

Don't even try. Ask him to appreciate that you are every bit as successful in your own way.

"Past relationships have broken up. How do I know this one won't?"

A pessimist sees the potential for break up, whereas an optimist sees the opportunity for a lovely, compatible relationship. Be optimistic!

"I think we're happy, so why do I still lack confidence?"

Make a conscious effort to act as though you are confident and you will become more and more self-assured.

"How can I maintain my self-esteem when he criticizes me?"

Point out that love supports and encourages whenever possible and never undermines self-esteem. Being a couple doesn't give the right to criticize each other.

"How can I stop feeling panicky about relationships. I tend to rush things and then make mistakes?"

Join the slow movement. Quietness and calm will let your confidence grow strongly and surely.

"I have a few traits I know aren't admirable, so how can I have self-esteem?"

Appreciate your good points and your character as a whole. Work on the things you don't like and start making positive changes.

"When I let my partner down why do I feel worse about it than he does?"

Because you're letting yourself down, too. For the sake of yourself, your partner and your relationship, stop doing it.

"How can I raise my self-esteem by changing my reactions to my partner?"

Behaving honestly and kindly, especially to your partner, will build your self-esteem hugely.

*"I'm hopeless at relationships.
How can I improve?"*

By realizing that your relationship can be
long lasting if both of you want it to be,
if you are compatible, and if you behave
lovingly to each other.

*"My partner often undermines
my self-esteem. How can I
bounce back?"*

Tell him to back off from trying to dent your
confidence. And remember your self-esteem is
precious, strong and deep.

**"I thought my partner would
make me happy and he does try,
so why aren't I?"**

*Happiness isn't something your partner can
engineer. It's an attitude of mind that starts
with self-esteem.*

"I'm trying to value myself highly, but how can I avoid seeming boastful?"

By keeping a sense of proportion and enjoying gently laughing at yourself and with others.

"Is there a way to increase our happiness individually and as a couple?"

Yes, if both of you do the things you're good at you'll feel good and be proud of each other too.

"Is self-approval helpful in a relationship?"

Yes, because it feels good, and how you feel reflects directly on your partner.

"Should I mix more with the friends who make me feel good?"

Yes. The company we keep has a big effect on our self-esteem, so make sure the impact is positive.

"A recent career setback has scared me. Supposing our relationship goes wrong too?"

Soothe and rationalize your fear by looking after your relationship lovingly and brightly to give it a strong foundation, and face any setbacks together supportively.

"How can I be confident about our love when I'm quaking inside about life generally?"

Because your love is sure and steady. Because you can deal positively with anything that goes wrong. Because you can take control of your attitude and reactions.

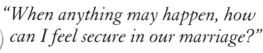

"When anything may happen, how can I feel secure in our marriage?"

By realizing that as you face change, you will adjust and make the changes necessary to cope.

"How can we raise each other's self-esteem?"

By identifying each other's good points and abilities, and pointing them out admiringly.

"Our low self-esteem is affecting our marriage. How can we improve both?"

Be glad for and praise each other's personality and talents. You'll raise each other's self-confidence and make your marriage a lovely place to be.

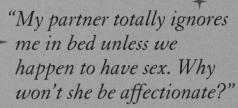

"My partner totally ignores me in bed unless we happen to have sex. Why won't she be affectionate?"

Perhaps she thinks you'll want sex when she doesn't or vice versa. Tell her it's nothing to do with sex, you just love to feel her touch and be close.

"When my partner's got a big meeting or presentation at work, how can I boost her confidence?"

Have steadfast faith in her and say: You'll be fine, you can do it.

"Can exercise help my self-esteem and can it benefit our relationship in any way too?"

Exercise within your present fitness limit will make you feel better, and your partner will be glad, for keeping fit is a compliment to her, too.

"Because we love each other, does it matter we're often not very nice to each other?"

Yes. Unkindness is a monster that suppresses each other's self-esteem. Stop it and be each other's best, most loving friend instead.

"How can I help restore my partner's self-esteem after he was made redundant?"

Tell him and show him you love him for who he is, not for his work.

"How can I best make my partner believe that she's a wonderful person?"

By telling her often that she is very special and you love her to bits.

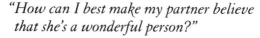

"My partner thinks his body's not up to much. How can I reassure him that I think he's fantastic?"

Tel him often, saying something like: *You've such an amazing body; you always look great.*

"What if my partner doesn't succeed at something?"

Reassure him that trying is the important thing and that he's a wonderful, valuable person whatever successes come or don't come his way.

"Can we help each other to be confident and happy in life generally?"

Yes, for love will even out life's path and, often, enable you to run and dance for joy.

"Is it healthy to be as competitive between ourselves as at work and in sport?"

Yes, if you both enjoy it, but no, if it deflates you. Most of all, be supportive of each other.

"My partner of ten years still looks at me with infatuation, which is gratifying but is it dangerous?"

It's great; continuing to see each other in a good, loving light is a sign of two pleased people and their happy marriage.

"Won't my partner get big-headed if I keep boosting his ego?"

No, he'll be thrilled you think well of him and will strive to live up to your expectations.

"How can we best help each other survive the competitiveness of our careers?"

Laugh together about yourselves and your professions so that you keep everything in perspective.

"There are many aspects of our lives where the other can't be involved. How can we prevent feelings of being left out?"

Telling each other about your respective lives will help you make sure that you both feel included and valued.

"Is it wise to offload the day's anxieties on each other?"

Yes, it's comforting to share the day's failures as well successes as long as it's within a reasonably short time limit.

"Is it normal to have doubts about the strength of our relationship?"

Yes. Most couples are fearful at times, and remember that facing any fears constructively will strengthen your love.

"We both have strong, quite different personalities. Should we try to tone down our characteristics so we're more similar?"

Love is about keeping your one-ness and respecting your partner's while moving comfortably alongside each other.

"Will it help our marriage if we both try to take a glass-half-full attitude?"

Yes. Seeing the good in each other and your relationship will boost each other's self-confidence and contentedness in the marriage.

"How can I show my partner I love him now just as much as the day we married?"

Think of all the things you did for and with him way back then, and do them now.

"Should I tell my partner what marriage means to me?"

Yes. How will she know, unless you do? And don't forget to ask her what marriage means to her.

"We still say the words, but how can I know for sure if my partner still loves me?"

Be more demonstrative yourself to encourage her to be as well. Words of love are great, but they're better still if they're backed up with loving actions.

"Why does our marriage feel vulnerable rather than strong?"

It needs you to build a strong framework of security with mutual reassurance of your love and commitment.

"Why does she worry more and more when I do all I can to hide problems from her?"

Partially hidden problems always seem scarier than they really are. Share worries with her, and you'll boost each other's confidence.

"Is it normal that I keep discovering new aspects of my partner?"

If often happens, even in the longest lasting relationships. Enjoy getting to know the whole, rounded person even better.

"We've stayed together for years, but more to maintain our lifestyle than love. How can I convince her this is normal?"

Why would you want to? Wouldn't it be nice to give her the love she yearns for and enjoy her love too? Give love all you've got.

"How can we most easily make the changes we need to in our relationship, such as arranging to spend more time together and reorganizing our household budget?"

With an organized approach and by being positive that the changes will go smoothly and increase your rapport.

"We don't pay each other much attention. Could he think we're staying together for the sake of the children?"

Perhaps, so talk about it and agree to put more into your relationship again. Increase the amount of attention you show each other and spell out with words and deeds your love and wish to be together for ever.

"Do I need to convince my wife, as I do my colleagues, that I'm more capable than I really am?"

No, no, no. Let down your guard and let her know and love the real you.

"What are the greatest compliments we can give each other?"

Trust and appreciation build self-esteem and confidence in each other.

"How can I most help my wife to do well in her career?"

To be constructively helpful you need to believe not only in her potential but also in her ability to fulfil it. Show her you believe in her, but don't push her.

"How can we give ourselves the confidence to mend our marriage?"

By stirring in daily quantities of commitment, kindness and self and mutual approval.

"We love being parents, but is it childish of me to wish my wife would call me by my name rather than Dad?"

To the kids it's fine to talk about you as *Dad*. Otherwise cherish your identity as lovers by using each other's names as well as endearments, like darling.

"How can I encourage my husband to appreciate me as a whole person rather than just as a mother and cook?"

Remind him that much as you like him complimenting you on these roles, you'd love it if he noticed all your facets.

"What would re-create a great vibe of confidence in our marriage?"

Looking for reasons every day to praise each other.

"It would make me feel more lovable if we spent more time together as a couple. What can we do?"

Set more time aside each week to go out together and aim to have at least some one-to-one time each day too.

"We know we need to repair our marriage, so why do we bury our heads in the sand and pretend it's ok?"

Because you're scared and idle. Be brave and put in the effort. Love is a million, million times worth looking after.

"Should I encourage my partner to opt for the security of the job he hates or make a move that could be risky?"

Don't push him either way but do encourage his self-esteem, and give him your full support whatever he does.

"When we stay in, my partner's always doing something on her own in her study. I feel unloved, but should I just accept it?"

Some time apart is fine, but part of the joy of being a couple is each other's company, so make a mutual decision to be together for several evenings a week.

"I know what I'm talking about, so why does my partner resist when I tell him how to do something better?"

It makes him feel incapable. Stop trying to control him and, unless he asks, don't keep giving him advice.

"My partner's feeling her age. How can I make her feel better?"

Tell her she's gorgeous and always will be.

"Does sex on TV make everyone's sex life seem dull?"

The contrast can be daunting! Boost your sexual self-esteem by telling each other you're wonderful lovers.

"When my partner says he's too tired to make love, am I neurotic to feel he's tired of me?"

Not neurotic but wrong! Agree another time when he won't be tired to make undemanding, non-exhausting, feel-good love.

"How can I restore my partner's sexual confidence after a period of ill health?"

Flirt with him undemandingly. Knowing that you find him attractive will do his self-esteem and sexuality the power of good.

"Can you recommend an easy way to give each other more enjoyment?"

Yes. Ask each other, *If you'd like one extra improvement to our lovemaking, what would it be?* and have fun implementing the answers.

"What's the best way to give each other sexual confidence?"

Let each other know you find them immensely attractive and show you do with lots of physical affection and by making love.

"Is it a normal woman thing that I feel used after sex?"

No one should ever feel used. Only have sex if you're both making love and showing love so you both feel loved and appreciated.

"How can I keep my sexual confidence when my partner makes excuses not to make love?"

Remind yourself that it isn't about you personally. Perhaps their sex drive is depressed or there's a relationship issue. Explore and address this together, lovingly.

"Can't I say I want to read or sleep rather than have sex without dashing my partner's ego?"

Yes, by agreeing roughly how often to make love and, when you do, compensating for a drop in quantity with mutual warmth and enthusiasm. This will reassure and raise both your egos.

"How can I convince my partner that every part of her body is just fine?"

By caressing her tenderly and telling her that she and every single part of her is adorable.

"How can I make him feel safe with me?"

Comment on how good you are together and he'll relax, knowing you think that you belong together.

"Should I pretend not to look at attractive people when I'm with my partner?"

You can't help noticing, but ogling them will annoy and perhaps dent your partner's belief in herself and you.

"However long my husband makes love to me, I don't climax. Am I just inadequate?"

Not at all. The apprehension of failing could be holding you back. You have the built-in ability and can learn the knack. Relax and enjoy.

"For my own self-esteem and my partner's as much as the pleasure factor, how can I learn to have an orgasm?"

Speak with your doctor about your concerns and you may be directed to some further professional advice. Also, there is plenty of good literature available; check in your library and on-line.

"My husband quite often doesn't want sex, even though I'm willing. Is it because I'm not attractive enough?"

No. Although a few men are testosterone charged to be up for it most of the time, most men are just like us; sometimes they feel like it, and sometimes they don't.

"I know my husband fantasizes when we make love. Should I feel jealous?"

No. Most people fantasize, but it's good manners to be discreet about it to protect each other's feelings.

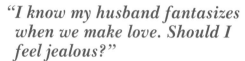

"Does my partner's penchant for soft porn mean I'm lacking something?"

No, it's nothing to do with you. It's a turn-on for some people no matter how much they love and fancy their partner.

"Why does my husband prefer to initiate sex?"

Some men love their partners to seduce them, others feel a bigger charge when he seduces you, and that's ok.

"Should we be bothered we don't have sex as often as friends do? Or do they just profess to for show?"

What they do or don't do is nothing to do with your lovemaking. All that matters is that you're both happy with it.

"Our encounters are not very fulfilling; should we see a sex therapist?"

That would be a sensible way forward; don't be embarrassed, it shows that you are concerned about keeping your relationship going.

"A friend's made me feel that we're failures by saying good lovers always climax together. Is it true?"

No, it's just a timing trick you can learn if you wish. But many prefer to take it in turns to climax so that they can fully focus on their own sensations.

"How can I get my husband to be a more confident lover without dashing his confidence?"

Lead him the way you want with your enthusiasm for what you like to do.

"My girlfriend is very routine in her lovingmaking. How can I liven things up?"

Gradually, gently, lovingly giving her lots of pleasure will encourage her to push her present boundaries and become a more pro-active lover. Compliment her often, too.

"Am I silly to get worried in between my partner's rare compliments that she doesn't rate me as much any more?"

No, we all need affirmation that we're doing ok. When she says something nice, tell her how much it means to you. It goes without saying that you should compliment her often.

"Is there a light-hearted way to make a difference to our rather static marriage?"

Play the what do we love about our marriage and would like more of game and promise to give each other whatever's mentioned.

Looking for love

& falling in love

"Can you really be attracted to someone across a crowded room?"

Oh yes!

"What causes love at first sight?"

An emotional and sexual response to a person's appearance, body language and pheromones.

"Is there a way we can make ourselves fall in love?"

You can't force yourself to fall in love, but a willingness to love and be loved and a genuine liking for the person certainly help foster it.

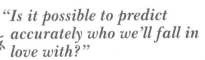

"Is it possible to predict accurately who we'll fall in love with?"

No. Although we may have an idea of the sort of person we're attracted to, chemistry can't be managed and may take us by surprise.

"Do you have to fancy a person to love them?"

To be in love with them, yes. To love them, not necessarily.

"Do you have to love a person to fancy them?"

No.

"Can I really have fallen in love
with him just by hearing his
voice on the phone?"

*Yes, because the sound of his voice and what he
says may be the expression of his soul.*

"He says my voice turns him on. Can sound do that?"

*The frequency and tenor of a voice can be
incredibly seductive. Usually, the lower the
pitch the sexier it is.*

"Are we more likely to fall in love in the spring?"

Yes. Spring is when we're most optimistic, happiest
and full of anticipation for the good things to come,
so we're well prepared to fall in love!

"When you're instantly attracted to someone, does it ever lead to lasting love?"

It may do if you find you like each other, get on well and have a lot in common.

"How can I make myself more attractive at first sight?"

Be confident that people like you and find you interesting, and make sure you like and take an interest in others.

"We're very much in love, but will the love last forever?"

Don't fret yourselves or threaten your present happiness by thinking of *for ever*. Cherish your time together now, and the future will take care of itself.

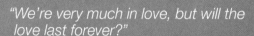

"He's not my type, but he is very rich. Is this enough for love?"

If it were, you wouldn't be asking the question. Besides, he would want you to love him for himself, not his wealth.

"Is there a reason we should try to keep romance alive even though we've been together for ages?"

Yes. It will add zest to your relationship and help keep your love strong and interesting.

"How can we be romantic when we've been together for years and know each other inside out?"

Romantic gestures, loving care and, now and then, an air of mystery will enrich your relationship forever.

"Is there a way to encourage my partner to be more romantic?"

Yes, by doing romantic things for her to give her the idea, and by being generous in your delight when she does something for you.

"Isn't it soppy and sentimental to give flowers and the like?"

It's part of the language of love. Don't be surprised if your partner enjoys those simple expressions of your love.

"What if we have different ideas about what's romantic?"

Alternate or mingle romantic gestures, bearing in mind what will please each other and showing understanding.

"How can I be extravagantly romantic when we're struggling to pay the bills?"

Forget financial extravagance. Love shows itself most romantically in the simplest ways.

"Any suggestions for non-materialistic, green romance?"

A single flower, little tea lights leading the way to your bed, messages of love hidden for your partner to find.

"What should we do if a romantic evening doesn't go according to plan?"

Laugh about it together and share the romance of fun.

"I buy my partner a card on Valentine's Day. Isn't that enough?"

It shows you've cared. But wouldn't it be lovely to show your love every day? Romance is so easy and will light up your life together.

"How can we be romantic without having to use material things?"

By looking into each other's eyes. A gentle caress. A kiss blown across a crowded room. There are a million ways to show your love!

"My best friend always seems to attract romantic partners. How can I encourage my new partner to be romantic?"

Bask with pleasure at any loving thing he says or does and tell him he's wonderful. He'll bask in your delight and praise, too, and want more of it!

"Do I need to try to meet someone new? Couldn't it happen romantically out of the blue?"

Yes, but you can improve the odds tremendously by providing yourself with opportunities.

"Statistically, where are you most likely to find love?"

Through work or friends' introductions and, increasingly, via introduction websites, newspaper columns and agencies.

"What are the most likely ways to meet someone compatible?"

Through your hobbies, interests, career or voluntary work.

"Isn't it unromantic to actively search for a partner and love?"

Keep an open mind and heart and a willingness to love and be loved and the search will be intrinsically romantic.

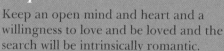

"Can I exaggerate my good points in my details for a dating site?"

Be positive but not inventive. You want anyone you meet to be pleased that you live up to your publicity!

"We've exchanged e-mails for ages, but he doesn't suggest phoning or meeting. What should I do?"

E-mail, Let's talk: when's good for you? *and arrange it. If he backs off, make more contacts who might be eager to get to know you in the real world.*

"Should I check if he's who he says he is?"

Yes, it's a vital precaution.

"How can I check him out when he's only given me a mobile phone number and says he works freelance on temporary jobs?"

If he's a genuinely nice, straightforward guy, he'll understand your concern and be happy to give you firm points of reference that prove his identity.

"I've fallen in love with him, but one or two things don't add up. I'm not sure that he is being truthful. Does this matter?"

Yes, it matters hugely. You're in love with an illusion and that's no good.

"We got on well in our e-mails, but when we spoke on the phone I didn't like his voice. Should we meet anyway?"

If you like what he says, go ahead. If you like him a lot the chances are that you'll get to like his voice too.

"I think he likes me, but he doesn't make a move. Should I?"

Yes, connection often needs a little encouragement.

"Do I ask him out, up front?"

If you want to and if it won't upset you if he declines, go ahead.

"Will he think I'm pushy if I ask him out?"

No. He'll be delighted you're confident.

"I'd like to suggest a date, but I know I'd be embarrassed if I asked him out and he said no. What can I do?"

Suggesting an outing as though he's a friend rather than a potential boyfriend will save embarrassment whatever happens.

"What's the most important thing to remember on a date?"

To focus on each other and not ogle or flirt with anyone else.

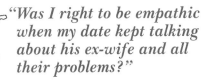
"Was I right to be empathic when my date kept talking about his ex-wife and all their problems?"

It was kind, but it's best not to get embroiled in each other's ex-partner baggage.

"My relatively new boyfriend unnecessarily lost his temper with a waiter and was noisily obnoxious. His conduct has put a real dampener on our relationship. Should I end it?"

Find out why he reacted so badly. Perhaps his explanation can help you understand and forgive him but make it clear that you will not tolerate such outbursts of unrestrained anger.

"I liked him, but his awkwardness and quietness on our first date embarrassed me. Should I see him again?"

Yes. He may be much more relaxed and talkative in future.

"My date kept bragging about herself. Is this a sign of arrogance or success?"

Either way, it's rude, but it could be due to shyness. Tease her gently if she brags again. With a bit of luck she'll take the hint and stop doing it.

"How should I act on a date?"

Take a warm interest in your date and be natural, open and kind.

"If I know I'm seriously interested in seeing my date again, should I show it?"

Yes, show your interest warmly, but don't throw yourself at her.

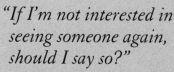

"If I'm not interested in seeing someone again, should I say so?"

The loving thing to do is to say, Thank you, I enjoyed our time together, so the date ends on a nice note, but doesn't give false hope.

"What's the most attractive thing about a new acquaintance?"

Genuine interest in each other. That goes for just about every relationship, actually!

"Is it rude to ask lots of questions?"

Some people think so, and it can feel like an interrogation, so don't ask zillions of questions and steer away from any very personal ones.

"How can I create a good atmosphere between us?"

Be pleasant and cheerful and don't complain about anything.

"I don't know a lot about etiquette and I don't want to embarrass my new date, who is much more sophisticated than I am. How can I avoid making gaffes?"

Follow his lead as far as things like table manners are concerned, and remember that he'll probably nervous too and aim to put him at their ease.

"Where's the best place for a first blind date?"

Meet in public, somewhere neutral.

"Should I dress up or wear everyday things?"

Wear something that's both becoming and comfortable so that you feel good and will be relaxed.

"We're good friends, but I want to be lovers! How do I find out if he too would like our relationship to change gear?"

Brush his arm with your hand, sit close to him on the sofa or drop sweet nothings into your conversation. He'll soon get the idea and, if his feelings match yours, start to respond.

"Is it important to impress him on our first date?"

Yes. You might want to see him again. So take care to look good and, of course, to be pleasant and charming. Your natural self, in other words!

"He apologized for not turning up for a date and was surprised I was upset. Should I see him again?"

It sounds as if he wasn't taught basic good manners, so give him another chance. If he's bright, he'll realize it's important to be considerate.

"My e-pal is flying in from abroad to meet me. How do we ease the inevitable pressure this puts us under?"

Decide to enjoy getting to know each other. That way it will be interesting and rewarding, and if a relationship sparks it will be a bonus.

"I think I like him, but how do I know he's not putting on a front?"

Be aware as you listen to him and watch his attitude to others.

"We get on well and like each other, but I want love. Could it still happen?"

Yes. Love often develops slowly, so enjoy this stage of your friendship as it grows and perhaps it will blossom into love.

"I don't want my new boyfriend to walk all over me like my last partner did. How can I show him I won't be a doormat?"

By valuing yourself and expecting him to regard you highly, too. If he is in any way patronizing or manipulating, show him the door.

"On the whole, I love him, but what about the flaws?"

Imagine how you'd feel about these if you were living together. If you couldn't accept them, accept you're not right for each other.

"I tend to make self-deprecating comments. How do I stop my new girlfriend teasingly putting me down the same way?"

Stop self-sabotaging and talk and act confidently and you'll stop inviting her to copy your disparaging remarks.

"We've fallen in love, but now I miss the mystery of not knowing how he felt about me. Is this usual?"

Enjoy your new intimacy, but keep surprising each other, too. Original thoughts and romantic touches nourish a sense of mystery and delight.

"How long does it take to get to know someone well?"

It depends how open he is and your own perspicuity. Some people let you get to know them quickly, with others it can take a lifetime or never happen.

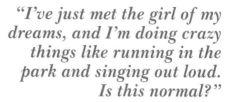

"I've just met the girl of my dreams, and I'm doing crazy things like running in the park and singing out loud. Is this normal?"

You are on a high and, yes, your symptoms are normal. You're in love. Enjoy!

"I really like my new friend, but I don't want to be hurt again. Is it necessary to be sceptical and hard?"

No. Be alert to and intolerant of any unkindness or thoughtlessness.

"We're so good together. Can we create love?"

Certainly, given attraction and compatibility.

"Can ongoing love always be spontaneous?"

It rarely is. Most of us need to choose to love, moment by moment, day by day.

"How do I know if the love I'm feeling is real or just infatuation?"

You can't for a while. Time will tell if it's lasting love, so stop worrying and enjoy it.

"I'm falling in love again. Can I steel myself against being hurt if it turns out to be infatuation?"

Yes, by realizing you'll soon recover if it's short lived. Enjoy it to the full, and you'll make lovely memories for the future, whether or not you stay together.

"I thought my new boyfriend was exactly right for me, but already flaws are showing up. Will I ever find someone perfect?"

Seeking perfection isn't fair or reasonable. No one could live up to your expectations.

"How long do I give a relationship before deciding if we love each other enough to continue with it?"

If you like each other a lot, take your time to get to know each other. Love's too important, too complex, to hurry.

"She worries frantically if I don't answer or return her too numerous calls. What can I do?"

Loosely agree an amount of contact that will suit you. Help her relax by being pleased to connect and taking your turn.

"My partner wants me with him so constantly it's claustrophobic. How can I break the pattern?"

Explain your need for independence.

"We're mad about each other
and want the feeling to last.
Is there any way it can?"

*The intense high is ephemeral, but romance
and love can continue to flower if you're good
together and want them to.*

*"Some say the in-love feeling lasts
for only a few weeks, others claim
that seven years is its usual
lifespan. Which is right?"*

It can dissolve in the blink of an eye,
at any stage, if you stop cherishing
each other.

"I really like him. Is that the same as love and is it enough?"

It's a kind of love. Whether it's enough depends on what you're both looking for in a relationship.

"Sometimes I look at him or think of him and feel as if I could melt with tenderness and happiness. Is this love?"

Yes, and isn't it just fantastic?

"I could only love him if he would change. Is it fair to ask him to?"

No. Although love is usually somewhat conditional, it doesn't stand much chance if you start out by making conditions.

"I'm lonely and my life is empty. Will meeting the right person transform my life?"

Possibly, but you'd be hugely dependent on her for your happiness. It's far better to find personal satisfaction and happiness so that you don't put pressure on your partner.

"He's wild about me but doesn't seem to notice that I'm less than in love with him. Would it be kind to tell him?"

If you're sure you've no future together, come clean and either agree to be just friends or part. It's not fair to keep him on a string.

"Either dates don't fall for me or vice versa. How can I make it happen?"

You can't, so stop fretting about it and enjoy taking an interest in everyone you meet without even contemplating whether or not this is it.

"He never gives me flowers or other gifts. Does it mean he doesn't really love me?"

No. He just hasn't acquired the habit. Try dropping hints or, better still, swap your individual lists of what represents romance and follow each other's lead.

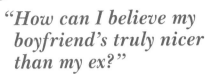

"How can I believe my boyfriend's truly nicer than my ex?"

If he's loving and caring to you, return the compliment in full. Active love like this leaves no room for old baggage.

"How can I stop falling for men who end up hurting me?"

Get to know and like the ones who are kind, uncomplicated and loving and give yourself permission to fall in love safely.

"I'm directionless and hard up. Would it make sense to look for a rich partner?"

No. For your own self-respect and inner satisfaction, make a plan and take steps to transform your life yourself.

"Even though he has given me no cause whatsoever to doubt him, why can't I trust my new boyfriend?"

You've been let down in the past, and your self-esteem is fragile. But most people are trustworthy, and it sounds as though your boyfriend is one of the good guys.

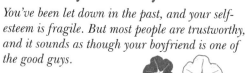

"We've both got lots of baggage. Will it snarl up our relationship?"

It could do. For the sake of your happiness as individuals and as a couple, address bad memories with shared understanding and perhaps with professional help. Then the past won't have a negative effect on the present.

"I love him but how can I stop longing for my ex?"

Imagine putting the longing into a box and snapping the lid on it. Now enjoy your present relationship to the full, and the out-of-date feelings will die.

"She's been married three times. If we marry is there any hope it will be permanent?"

Yes, if you're both willing to pay attention to your love and care for it well.

"How will I know when I meet the right one?"

You'll feel it in your bones, and your heart will sing.

"How do we take it from infatuation to lasting love?"

Realize that it's not just sexual attraction and enjoy the contentment you've found together.

"Do we need to have a formal engagement?"

It's up to you whether to have a formal engagement. It's a good excuse for a party!

"Is it normal to be scared of losing my freedom?"

Yes, but you won't if you appreciate each other's respective need for personal space.

"I'd like a big wedding with all the trimmings, but my fiancé says it's a waste of money. What do I do?"

Have your special day but show mutual respect by compromising with fewer guests, for instance, or a less expensive dress, venue or meal.

"When's the right time to buy a house together and perhaps get married, too?"

When you're both sure you intend to stay together and want to pledge your love.

"Should I insist that my new husband wears a wedding ring like me?"

No. It's a symbol of commitment, but it's always a personal choice.

"Why would we make a commitment?"

For an element of emotional and financial security, and because when you love each other it's often the natural mutual wish.

"I love her to bits, but some things about her are annoying. Will they spoil our love?"

No one's perfect, even you, and love is about getting on together, faults and all.

"My boyfriend wants to buy
me a diamond engagement ring.
Should I say I'd rather have my
preferred semi-precious stone?"

*Yes. Rings are very symbolic, and it's important for
your love and relationship that he values your
opinions and choices.*

*"We've been going out together
for years and love each other
deeply, so why does he shy away
from marriage?"*

Ask him and discuss what it would
mean to you both.

"Does it matter if she refuses to marry me, even though we live so happily together?"

Not as long as you accept her stance and have discussed financial and long-term security issues to protect yourselves.

"I'm very fond of him, but he's terribly boring. Will he drive me mad eventually?"

Yes and this will only get worse. Someone else might find him scintillatingly interesting, so free him so that he can find her.

"After only three weeks, should I let him move in with me?"

State your reservations and let your love and mutual understanding develop slowly, keeping your own territories to retreat to for a while.

"He says he doesn't want commitment or children, and I want both. What now?"

You're priorities are unlikely to change, but his may, so give him a little more time.

"Must I stop seeing other men if we agree to go steady?"

Probably yes. But talk about what commitment means to you both to save misunderstanding.

"We're too young to settle down yet, but I don't want either of us to sleep with other people. Is this reasonable?"

Perfectly. It's normal to be monogamous while you're going out together unless you agree otherwise.

Getting on together

"Is it normal sometimes to be irritated by the person you love so much?"

Yes. No matter how much you love each other, you'll almost certainly lose patience with each other from time to time.

"How can I stop him taking it for granted I'll run errands for him?"

Agree a fair and regular division of tasks, or opt to decide who does what as the need arises. Also agree that every task will be willingly done and generously appreciated.

"Should I tell my girlfriend when she gets on my nerves?"

If it's trivial, or more about you than her, let it go. Otherwise, you could say, I'm feeling irritated because…. A problem aired can be resolved.

"Am I wrong to be hard on my partner because I don't want her to treat me in the same way my previous girlfriend did?"

It's far better to encourage loving behaviour with trust and appreciation than to make hard demands. Let go of your past bitterness so that it doesn't affect your present love.

"I find it infuriating when he's late. Is he right to retort that I'm over-reacting?"

Repeated tardiness and the way he patronizes your anger suggest passive aggression. Help him to resolve the causes so that this doesn't sabotage your love.

"I've begged him to give up smoking. If he loves me he should, shouldn't he?"

Whatever the rights and wrongs of smoking, it's never right to force someone to do something for you for love's sake. Love is not a lever or a bargaining tool.

"How can I stop being irrationally annoyed by little things about my boyfriend?"

Immediately you sense a small irritation contain it, then let it go and focus on something you love about your partner.

"Some things about my boyfriend are never going to change. Will they always irritate me?"

Not if you remember that you love him, warts and all.

"We've been advised to talk about our problems, but how can we do this when we're mad at each other?"

Agree to talk about the problems when you've both cooled down, then look at the difficulty calmly and rationally.

"We've just been arguing about science vs. religion. What should we do when we feel poles apart like this?"

Remember that it's fine to have different opinions. What matters is that you love each other.

"Is it normal to hate your partner when you're in the middle of a row?"

Yes, that is, you feel as though you hate them. Love hasn't died though, it's just been temporarily eclipsed by an excess of negative emotion.

"How do I respond if my boyfriend refuses to change his bad habits when I nag him to?"

Asking him in another way or moderating your request might encourage him to be more willing.

"Is there a non-confrontational way to sort out a dispute?"

Yes. The loving way is to focus on finding solutions together, instead of criticizing and accusing each other.

"Is it better not to row?"

Yes. Harsh words and insults can do lasting damage, even when you didn't really mean them.

"Why does it make me cringe when he's sarcastic?"

Because sarcasm shows his pain and it hurts you too. Make it your mutual aim to solve grievances fairly, kindly and constructively.

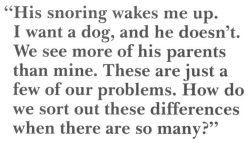

"Surely it's more healthy to express anger than to swallow it?"

Yes, but there is no need to shout or be nasty. Think how you can let off steam another way, and only address the problem that's troubling when you're thinking clearly and calmly.

"His snoring wakes me up. I want a dog, and he doesn't. We see more of his parents than mine. These are just a few of our problems. How do we sort out these differences when there are so many?"

Thinking about them all at once will be too overwhelming. Tackle the problems one at a time, working as a team, and if you adopt a combination of love and logic you'll eventually overcome them all.

'How do our friends manage to get on well all the time when we're often annoyed with each other?'

They probably find the best way to address their problems (we all have them) purposefully when they are at home, so that they can enjoy the rest of their time together.

"I met my boyfriend recently and just know that he is the one for me. How can I make sure that we will always enjoy each other's company this much?"

Remember to share each other's company and never forget what it was that brought you together, and enjoy being together!

"I seem to get on better with my friends than with my boyfriend. What can I do to reverse this?"

Be as comforting, inspiring and interesting together as you are with your friends, and make sure you have as much fun with your boyfriend as you do with them.

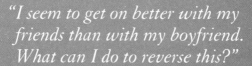

"I'm slightly in awe of my clever partner and find it hard to relax when she's so much brighter than I am. What should I do?"

Think of how much you love each other and your tension will disappear.

"We love each other, but should we be anxious about sharing a home?"

No, not if you think of living together as an extension of loving together.

"What's the most important element of living together?"

Thinking of your relationship as being your home.

"I'm moving in with my boyfriend, but he's complaining about how much stuff I'm bringing with me and says that I'm suffocating him. How can we fit everything in?"

Keep the things that please you a lot and give away everything else, including any superfluous gadgets and kitchen equipment.

"Our meals together always end in a row because my girlfriend brings up sensitive topics. How can we stop ourselves spoiling mealtimes by talking about upsetting things?"

Rule out talk about money and any other subjects that are likely to rile you. Mealtimes are for peace and enjoyment.

"I want to move in with my girlfriend, but we both have strong egos. Will we get along in a small space?"

Yes, if you love and respect each other.

"As we agreed, I take care of domestic decisions, so how should I react when my partner buys a piece of furniture without consulting me?"

He fell in love with it, so opt to do the same; he'll adore you for your generous acceptance.

"Should we share the interior decorating, even though I'd rather do it myself?"

If she's keen to be involved, yes. Remember it's her home too.

"I have moved in with my girlfriend and find myself spending money I don't have to support her expensive lifestyle. When I complain, she says I'm being unreasonable. What should I do?"

Talk this problem through calmly and carefully with her, matching incomings and outgoings. When everything is set out on paper in a non-confrontational way, she may well accept your point of view.

"We don't share the same taste in interior design, so how shall we do up our house?"

Every couple has to sort this out in their own way. You could compromise, or take turns to do a room, or, if you plan to move often, the whole house. Alternatively, let whichever of you is more passionate about a choice make it.

"My parents tease me about my boyfriend, who is really very nice, and about our relationship. Should I defend our love?"

Yes. Tell them that they're over the top and say, Ok, the fun's over. It's time to stop the joshing.

"Our daughter is dangerously ill and the stress is driving us apart. How can we keep our love intact?"

Guard carefully the sense that you're a partnership united by your love and that you wish to be together at this difficult time.

"Apart from her refusal to dance and her shyness in company, I really like my girlfriend. How can I stop these characteristics from putting me off?"

Accept her preference not to dance, it's a free country, after all. Accept her shyness, too, and gently encourage and support her as she learns to relax more.

"We're a bit like children: sometimes great mates, other times squabbling. Is this all right, or should we aim for total harmony?"

Ups and downs are inevitable in any relationship, and they're no bad thing, because as your understanding of each other grows, you love will grow stronger.

"Should we ignore, tolerate or try to squash each other's eccentricities? For example, I like to have conversations with the cats, and he wears crazy shirts."

As each other's nearest and dearest, gently point it out to each other if a foible is beginning to look deranged rather than simply quirky. In general, though, be lovingly tolerant.

"How can we be assertive about our individual needs without fighting?"

If, as a team, you do your best to help make sure that each other's needs are met, you'll be working together, and there will be no need to fight.

"When one of us has an angry outburst, the other responds with immediate anger too. How can we break this cycle?"

At any moment, the decision to react with anger or understanding insight is the choice you and your partner make. Take the path of understanding.

"If I don't react angrily to his bad temper, how can I stop him bullying me?"

Provide the firm boundaries and understanding he needs with the calm strength and dignity of your refusal to be bullied or lose your temper.

"Should I be rigid about what I want?"

No. In general, a varying degree of flexibility is the key to satisfactorily meeting your needs.

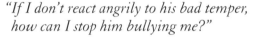

"To be honest, we actually enjoy a row now and then: it lets off steam and we usually have fantastic sex afterwards. Are fights such a bad thing?"

If you both love the zest they add to your relationship they're fine. Don't be horrid to each other, though, it could wear thin one day.

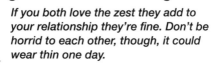

"Is there a good recipe for harmony?"

Yes. Be intuitive about each other and easy-going yourselves.

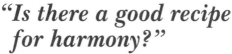

"My husband says my faith and quest for spirituality are a fantasy. Is he right?"

Rather than telling you that you're wrong (and after all how can he possibly know?) the loving thing to do would be to respect each other's beliefs.

"When I lost my job recently, I said, **Not to worry, I'll find another one soon,** *but he fretted about our finances. Is it better to be an optimist like me or a pessimist like him?"*

Taking a positive stance feels much better and will help you react constructively, but he's the way he is, so appreciate his opinions and support each other.

"When things go well I bounce about exuberantly, much to my girlfriend's irritation. Should I tone it down for our love's sake?"

No, don't squash your happiness, but do be empathetic and supportive if she is feeling down.

"Should I bend my political views to his as he thinks I should?"

No. Love doesn't try to control or impose opinions; it understands the other's right to make up their own mind.

"My husband is such a party-pooper. How can I get him to enjoy celebrations?"

Ask him to have a go at sharing your pleasure next time you're on top of the world. If he goes along with it for even a few minutes he'll probably enjoy it and be ready to have fun more often.

"There's no joy in my marriage. We've tried hard to make it work, but that's all our marriage is: hard work. Would it make sense to give up and separate?"

The hardest part often comes just before a major breakthrough, and your love may be on the brink of regeneration. So try again, maybe with different tactics, to get on well.

"My girlfriend says some mean things to and about me. Is this acceptable?"

No, it's destructive and horrid, so refuse to tolerate it and together explore what's behind her unhappiness.

"If my girlfriend wants to go clothes shopping and I don't, should I go with her to avoid a row?"

No. Stand up to the threat, so that she realizes that she shouldn't try to control you like this. However, most people join their partner as a loving gesture from time to time, even though it's not something they would have chosen to do alone.

"How can I stop my girlfriend from throwing whatever I say back at me when we argue?"

Try looking fairly and honestly at your own actions and words as well as at hers, and then take time to discuss this with her.

"Why is everything always my fault?"

Try being gentler and more thoughtful to ease your partner's aggressive defensiveness. And help him develop the self-confidence to shoulder the blame or to be understanding when something goes wrong.

"My partner sometimes makes me cry when we argue, then hates it when I do. Should I try not to?"

No. Be careful not to make each other cry, but ask him to respond to your tears with acceptance, comfort and support.

"I know I'm sometimes picky for no reason. Should we accept it's just the way I am?"

No. This is not something to be proud of, and it's so easily changed. When you notice yourself being unfairly edgy, deliberately be pleasant instead and enjoy the warm glow it gives you as well as your partner.

"My marriage is floundering and we've ignored our problems for years. Is it too late to solve them?"

If you're both willing, it's never too late.

"He thought his sister was rude yesterday; I thought she was wittily outspoken. Why do we see things so differently?"

Reality is often subjective. Try stepping into each other's shoes and imagining the situation from the other's viewpoint.

"I'm losing patience with my partner. I'm a glass-half-full person, but my partner always sees the down side and my bright outlook annoys him. Should I dim it?"

And wallow in gloom together? No, continue to enjoy life to the full. It's contagious. He can choose to be upbeat and optimistic if he wants.

"When we're in company, my partner draws attention to my faults. Should I just accept this?"

No, it's unloving and bad form. Sort out your differences in private.

"Every time we have a row my girlfriend digs up memories of past fights, which makes things worse. How can we stop escalating rows by digging up these memories?"

Remind each other to focus on the disagreement that you're trying to resolve today.

"Why does my girlfriend pick on me all the time?"

Perhaps she learned the habit from her parents (in which case it's time to stop perpetuating it) or perhaps there's a problem you need to talk about and resolve.

"I find our arguments exhausting. How can we stop goading each other to lose control and shout or cry?"

By helping each other retain dignity and talking together to find and agree a solution.

"My girlfriend says we're both impossible to live with, but is it unrealistic to think we can change?"

If you want to change for the better and are prepared to put in whatever effort it takes, you can do so, especially with each other's support.

"Will it put my partner off me if I admit that I have a problem with anger and want to deal with it better?"

I expect he already knows about it and will be pleased you want to deal with it.

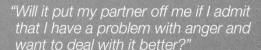

"I regret the affair I had and can't see the point of raking over it as my girlfriend wants to. Will talking about it make us close or drive us apart?"

As long as neither of you is accusatory, the intimacy of addressing the various issues will broaden your mutual understanding, draw you closer and enable you both to move on.

"It upsets my partner if I'm angry. Should I pretend I'm not?"

No. Help him see it's a natural emotion and not wrong in itself. Make an effort to learn to deal with your own and each other's anger thoughtfully and safely.

"My parents were always arguing. How can I avoid repeating history so that we can be one of those couples who never disagree?"

Some conflict is a given for two strong-minded people, no matter how much they love each other, so relax and deal with it sensibly.

"When we have differences I feel like divorcing. How can I stop over-reacting?"

Accept that you're bound to have differences, and either live comfortably together despite them or do something to remedy them.

"My partner has a short fuse and shouts at me. Should I shout back?"

No, it's best definitely not to do so. Instead you should choose to deal constructively with the attack or leave the room until you are both calm enough to discuss the problem rationally.

"My partner keeps bullying me. What should I do?"

Match her aggression with your own strength of character, expressing it calmly and showing clearly that you are no longer going to be a victim.

"My girlfriend keeps bringing up quite understandable grievances from our past. We're both much nicer people now, but how can I convince her to let go?"

Agree to forgive each other for old hurts and consign them to the dustbin so they don't poison your togetherness today.

"Why won't my partner see things the way they really are, even when I spell it out to her?"

Don't assume you're always right. Take in and respect each other's opinions.

"He says I don't listen, but why should I when I know exactly what he's going to say?"

Because it's rude, because you're probably mistaken anyway, and because he feels desperately neglected. Always listen to each other with fresh interest.

"When she nags me to do things I just dig in my heels and refuse. How can I stop her driving us apart this way?"

Talk about the pattern you're both in and meet halfway, so instead of nagging or criticizing each other, listen politely to what the other has to say and, whenever possible, willingly help out with the task.

"Is there one ingredient that can make a failing relationship good again?"

Yes, love. Pro-active love, that is.

"Should I tolerate my partner's rudeness?"

Only if she is suffering from dementia, in which case seek help. Between two healthy adults rudeness is unacceptable and dangerous, because love thrives in an atmosphere of mutual kindness and politeness.

"I am growing away from my boyfriend of four years. How can love help hold us together when we're growing apart?"

Renew the habit of behaving lovingly to each other, and you will grow back together.

"We share a house but lead separate lives. Has our love died?"

Love can hibernate in a cold climate. Lavish attention and love on each other, and the warmth will reactivate it.

"He says I never tell him anything. Do I need to tell him everything?"

Keeping each other informed about what's going on in both your individual and your shared life will show that you value each other and make you feel like a team.

"She says I'm patronizing. What does she mean?"

You're talking down to her or giving the impression that you're cleverer or better informed. Cut it out!

"He threatens he'll leave if I mention something that's worrying me about our relationship. Should I just back off as I always have?"

That won't solve anything, so tell him you're not criticizing him but need to share, discuss and address relationship issues together.

"Am I silly to be hurt because my wife cooks amazing meals for our friends but gets take-aways or opens cans when we're on our own?"

Sharing lovingly prepared food is such a pleasure, but she's just got into a routine of preparing fast food. Mention how you feel to her, and work out together how you can enjoy home cooking, perhaps taking turns more often. You're both worth it!

172 GETTING ON TOGETHER

"What are the main qualifications for a great relationship?"

There are many qualities, but they all start with the wish to love and let love be.

"My boyfriend is very careful and measured, and it drives me mad. Surely love should be spontaneous?"

It's often spontaneous, but it's often chosen, too. Either way you need to be loving, whether it's spontaneously or thoughtfully.

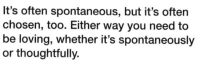

"Does it matter that we both have different ideas on the meaning of love?"

Not if you are loving to each other. Love has many meanings, but common to all is loving conduct.

"My boyfriend wants to make a long-term commitment, but I'm worried that we will fall out of love. If we change as we mature, will we still love each other?"

Yes, if you accept that as two naturally developing people you can adjust your relationship as needed.

"I think love comes into everything, but my boyfriend thinks it's mostly about sex. I feel disappointed, but do our differing views really matter?"

Yes, because disappointment is serious. Perhaps he does love you more generally than he realizes. Does he behave lovingly and considerately? If he does, recognizing this may be all it takes for both of you to realize all the love you long for is there, after all.

"Why do we sometimes push each other's buttons almost as though it's intentional?"

Because you can! Agree with each other not to do this, and make it a habit to boost each other's confidence instead.

"Should I follow my mother's example of going icily quiet when she and my father had a dispute?"

No. Love is being there for each other in ups and downs, and warmth heals hurts and seals mutual forgiveness.

"I feel frustrated because my partner doesn't want me to turn my hobby into my living. Why is she so negative?"

She's scared. Ask her to help you live your dream, but soothe her fears with well-researched business and contingency plans.

"I follow the saying, *Never apologize, never explain*, but my girlfriend gets cross with me because I never do either. Should I change?"

Definitely. In most relationships, especially a loving one, it's great to be prepared to clear confusion and if you're in the wrong to admit it and apologize.

"My partner's keen on relationship books, but won't it seem false if we do things by a book?"

There's no need to copy everything a book says, but picking up a few tips that are appropriate for your particular relationship can be useful. Don't worry: you're two unique people, so your relationship will always be unique too.

"Can we relax now we're sure of each other?"

Yes, but always keep your eyes open to see the love between and all around you and actively enjoy it.

"We're so considerate and polite to each other that our life together sometimes seems a bit cold and distant. How can we warm up our relationship?"

Make and grab opportunities to play and laugh, and get involved with something you both love. Connection takes practice, but it will soon become wonderfully natural.

"Is there an aspect of love that's more apparent and precious later in life?"

Yes. You've the time and wisdom to appreciate each other's presence. You turn round and your partner's there, and that's a beautiful thing.

"Do we need to fix occasional petty quarrels?"

No. All couples have them, and usually they're caused by tiredness and are best forgotten.

"We work, look after the children and sleep. How can we do something about the emotional desert that is our relationship?"

Take the time and make the effort that love needs if it is to thrive. It's the best thing you'll ever do.

"So far we've sorted out in-law and financial problems. Will there always be something going wrong?"

Probably, but the more you learn about problem-solving and loving each other, the more often your relationship will purr happily along.

"We know each other so well that I'm scared it could become boring. Does familiarity cause love to go stale or to grow?"

Because you know each other well, your love will grow in intimacy and never stale as long as you take a vibrant interest in each other.

"We seem to bounce from dealing with one of life's problems to another. Won't it become tedious to do nothing but manage career and domestic problems, no matter how satisfying that is?"

Absolutely. So make time to appreciate and actively enjoy the good times and romance together, as they're every bit as important as the problems you encounter.

"My boyfriend says I'm selfish. How can I show him I'm not?"

Do a little something unexpected every day for him that will bring a smile to his face.

"I think my girlfriend equates love with the high life. How can we afford to keep love alive on a budget?"

Share the simple pleasures of each day. Feasting on bread and cheese and relaxing afterwards can be sheer heaven if you enjoy the togetherness.

"In the long term, do we need more than occasional moments of exquisite oneness?"

Yes. Take the time in between to develop trust, to learn about each other's character and to maintain and enjoy a well-rounded relationship.

"Now our lifespans are so much longer, is it realistic to think a marriage can last a lifetime?"

Cynics say it's unrealistic, but they're wrong as it's unquestionably possible because so many couples are vibrantly happy after many, many decades together. Mostly, they put it down to being loving, flexible and enthusiastic. Like happiness, love needs us to take part.

Communication

"If we talk lovingly more often, will we understand each other better?"

Yes. It's a kind of magic when you put love into words because it helps you both realize how you feel.

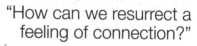

"How can we resurrect a feeling of connection?"

Begin by starting to talk and listen to each other again.

"Neither of us is big on talking. Are there other ways to keep in touch?"

Yes. Do things together, take an interest in each other's experiences and be demonstratively loving.

"We can't talk to each other any more. Why is this and what can we do?"

Like any neglected habit, talking can be difficult to start up again. Make the effort and then practise, practise, practise, and it will soon become not only easy again but a real pleasure.

"Like her parents, my partner's not demonstrative. Can she learn to be?"

Yes, and as she gets used to enjoying your language of love, she'll want to speak it herself.

"My partner's more articulate than I am, so how can I hope to hold my own in an argument unless I shout?"

Discover the power of pausing to think. It will enable you to say what you want, clearly, surely and evenly.

"Can too much talk be depressing?"

Yes, if it's mostly negative. Aim to lift each other's spirits by talking about all the good things and feelings in your lives.

"When's the best time to talk?"

Loving words in the morning warm you all day and, in the evening, mutual loving attention makes you feel special. Any time is good, though.

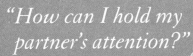

"How can I hold my partner's attention?"

By giving her yours.

"Is there a way to encourage him to be loving?"

Yes. Be clearly appreciative when he is.

"Is it good to talk every day?"

There are no set rules, but being able to talk things over with someone who loves you and isn't judgmental or controlling is one of the great blessings of a loving relationship.

"How do I get my thoughts across to my partner?"

If you're enthusiastic and positive, you'll be naturally eloquent.

"Isn't it a bit saccharine to keep saying nice things?"

Far better sweet than sour.

"How can I convince him I am listening?"

By looking at him and gesturing you're hearing him with facial expression or, if he can't see your face, by murmuring agreement, sympathy and so on as he speaks.

"Why is he so defensive, often aggressively so? For instance, I only have to mention something he's done and he assumes I'm criticizing him."

He feels out on a limb. Show him you're on his side and build his self-confidence by telling him you agree with or feel the same as him whenever you do.

"Is it best to ignore it if my partner's in a bad mood?"

No, saying something to show you've noticed and asking if there's anything you can do to help will mean a lot.

"Isn't it enough that my partner knows I love her?"

Never assume that your partner knows you love her. Tell her and show her you do.

"Is it ok to be loving in front of others?"

It's excellent because, as well as being nice for the two of you, others will be pleased you value each other.

"Should I hide it or talk about it when I feel down?"

Talk. It gets it off your chest, enables you to address what's wrong and gives your partner the chance to be supportive.

"Can talk be dangerous for love?"

Yes, very, so beware of using words against each other.

"Will talking make us closer?"

Yes, for when you talk kindly together your minds hold hands.

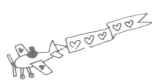

"Why is communication so important?"

It's the heartbeat of a relationship that sends love flowing through everything you do and are together.

"Is there an instant way to communicate something without necessarily talking?"

Yes. A hug can say Hi *or* Au revoir, *convey affection or empathy, say* thank you *or* I'm sorry, *forgive, make peace. And hugging shows you care.*

"She says it's often difficult to keep in contact when she's away on business. Should I press her to?"

Yes. All it takes to phone or text or write a letter is love, and it gives such a lot of joy.

"We no longer talk about our love. Does it matter?"

Yes, because words of love highlight and reaffirm your love and will make you both feel good.

"Is there any kind of communication we should avoid?"

Yes. Scathing criticism, sarcasm, put downs, rough touch, unkind ways: all these are the antithesis of love.

"How can we stop being rude to each other?"

Think and behave lovingly and with mutual respect.

"How can I enjoy talking when experience has taught me that words are dangerous?"

Agree to use words as messengers of mutual understanding and peace.

"Should we have a special way of talking to each other?"

Yes, speak to each other as though you are very special and important. You both are. Let love flow through what you say and the way you say it.

"How can we make sure that our talk is helpful and positive?"

Speak from the heart with love in mind.

"Why is my partner dismissive and embarrassed when I'm nice to her?"

Sadly, she's not learned to receive compliments gracefully and enjoy the mutual benefits of loving actions.

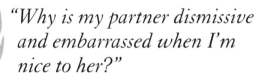

"How can I help her enjoy endearments and loving gestures?"

Tell her the joy it will give you to know you give her pleasure, and help her try being appreciative. Encourage her to be lovingly demonstrative to you in turn.

"How can I know when something I've said or done has unintentionally upset my partner if she doesn't tell me?"

Feel it when you hug, listen between the lines of what she says and read her body language. Love notices things in many ways. Ask her gently, as well, to be open with you about anything that has bothered her.

"My partner sometimes needs some quiet time to himself: is that ok?"

Yes, it's fine. Most of us need time to ourselves, for example, for private reflection and creativity.

"Why won't he talk to me any more?"

Behind his passive resistance is hurt or a feeling of helplessness. Tackle the roots together and change your pattern of talking so that it's positive and forward-going.

> *"Is there a method to talking well, in the sense of throwing light on problems or issues between us?"*

Yes. We need to express what we want to say clearly, focus on listening to each other and check we've heard right. Misunderstanding flees and love thrives where there's clarity and shared understanding.

"Should I ignore the vicious things my partner shouts at me?"

Ignoring what he says could be difficult because harsh words are powerful weapons. It would be best for both of you to find out why he shouts abusively and to resolve the problem so he never does it again.

"It's questions, questions, questions. How can I stop my partner giving me the third degree?"

Make sure you talk to her responsively so she doesn't feel cut off. If she still cross-questions you, point out the habit gently.

"My partner manipulates me into waiting on her, for instance by pointedly saying, *I'd love a cup of tea.* How can I stop her surreptitiously getting me to do things without directly asking me?"

Explain how it feels to be frequently manipulated and agree to be direct with each other.

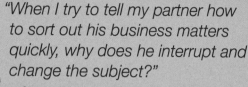

"When I try to tell my partner how to sort out his business matters quickly, why does he interrupt and change the subject?"

Appreciate that he wants to handle them himself and let him.

"We're never apart for long, so why does my wife need to talk when we get together?"

She needs to feel reconnected. A loving How's it going? or All well?, followed by interest in your respective answers will show that you care about each other's wellbeing.

"Is talk really so important?"

Important? It's vital. It's the chance for two people who know each other intimately and deeply to communicate lovingly and understandingly.

"Is it important to be honest if there's a problem in our relationship?"

Yes. Unaddressed problems spoil and even destroy relationships. Facing them together enables you to resolve them.

"Should I be honest if I don't like the outfit my partner's wearing, or is it best to fib?"

It's better to choose tact, silence or truth. Lies can cause distrust.

"Can words heal?"

Yes. Loving words, like I love you, Let me help you, *I'm sorry and* I think you're wonderful, *are precious, healing balm.*

"Does it matter that according to my partner I don't sound pleased when I answer his phone calls?"

It matters hugely, because the way you say hello can dash or lift his spirits and your love for each other. Be delighted to hear his voice and show it, clearly, in yours.

"Should I say I love you when my partner rarely says it to me?"

Yes. Saying I love you is a lovely thing to do and hear, and it doesn't necessarily need to be responded to in kind.

"Should I tell him my ideas, fears, hopes and so on?"

Yes. How can he ever know you if you don't?

"Can talking help each other's dreams come true?"

Yes. If you listen to each other's heart's desires you may help each other along the path towards them.

*"My boyfriend calls me several times a day, and sometimes I find myself thinking, **Oh no, not again.** Can I tell him I'd rather he didn't phone so often?"*

No. It might hurt his feelings and put him off calling you at all. Think how much you love him and be glad he loves to contact you. Remember, you don't have to answer every time; then, when you do, you'll be genuinely pleased to speak with him.

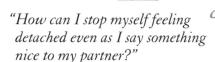

"How can I stop myself feeling detached even as I say something nice to my partner?"

When you say something connect with your facial expression and body language, as they're as or more important than the words.

"How can we find time and a quiet place to talk?"

Agree to make time, or just switch off the TV or computer and go for a drive or walk together.

"What can we talk about after so many years together?"

Anything and everything, everyday things and topical issues: the more you do it, the easier and more enjoyable it becomes.

"How can we create a deeper connection between us?"

Be sensitive to each other's wellbeing and emotions and be warmly supportive.

"She doesn't listen to me, so I've stopped talking. Why doesn't she realize why I'm quiet?"

Tell her you used to feel hurt when she didn't listen, and make a pact together to focus fully on what the other says and enjoy your conversations.

"Although we talk lots, we often misunderstand each other completely. How can this be?"

Words can mean different things to different people, and sentences are often ambiguous too.

"How can we make sure we understand what has been said?"

Take care when you're choosing words and get into the habit of repeating what you think you've heard to check you've understood correctly.

"The other day, he said, Why can't you just listen? but why shouldn't I give advice?"

Sometimes all we want is for our partners to hold our thoughts and feelings. That's fine.

"Is it ok to chatter spontaneously to my partner, even though I sometimes thoughtlessly say something insensitive as the words flow?"

With her more than anyone, choose words with care and love, for they carry yourself to her, and you don't want to be misunderstood or to hurt her.

"Why does he balk when I ask him to do something?"

In case he sees direct requests as demands, take a gentle approach, such as starting with *Darling have you got time to…?* or *Do you think you could possibly…?*

"Why does she get so aggressive when we disagree?"

She feels you're scorning her opinions. Show her you respect her views by listening carefully and valuing them.

"Why is it we can sometimes talk things through constructively but at other times we end up rowing?"

Your ability to be positive is influenced by your body clocks. Pick a time of day when you both feel awake and bright.

"My partner says I don't listen, but how can I find time?"

Prioritize.
Listening = paying attention = love.

"How can we stop talking endlessly around something and instead find out what's really wrong so we can solve it?"

Be brave and go to the heart of the question. The solution will follow.

"Are there any no go *times for serious conversation?"*

Yes, mealtimes and any time you're tired or in a negative mood.

"I don't mean to stone-wall my partner, but how can I explain that my brain goes into overload when we've talked for ages?"

Say, I'm exhausted. Can we talk about this again later please? *so she knows you're not abandoning the conversation.*

"How can I get my partner to understand what I'm saying instead of hearing what he wants to hear?"

Slow down your conversation and play back each other's words, by beginning with *So what you're saying is ...* to prevent misunderstandings.

"How do I tell my partner what I feel is wrong without making her hostile?"

Stating your complaint simply with no personal criticism will avoid her feeling threatened or unloved.

"Should I pretend I know how I'm feeling when I don't?"

No, be honest and say, I don't know *to avoid misunderstanding.*

"What's the most important thing to avoid when we're discussing a problem?"

Contempt of each other. You're together because you love each other; always, always, always remember this.

"When I ask my partner his opinion, about how I look, for instance, he dodges the question. How can I make him realize that prevaricating doesn't protect me but just annoys me?"

Tell him how you feel and agree to give each other straight answers.

"How can my partner say I'm being difficult when I often don't say anything?"

Check out your body language. It can express negative emotions, such as scorn and irritation, as clearly as any words.

"If something's bothering me, the way my partner is tackling a DIY job, for example, how should I tell her the way I want it done?"

Don't snap a criticism. Simply and directly say what it is that is worrying you about her handiwork and, if it's helpful, how you would like her to do it.

"Why is love never straightforward for us?"

Love is simple, but we complicate it. Asking yourself, What's the loving thing to do right now? will help a lot.

"Are there any words to avoid?"

Yes, *always* and *never* sound accusing and daunting. If you want to make a point it's better to say, I *feel you don't often…* or *I'd really appreciate it if you could sometimes…*

"We talk a lot, so why doesn't it help?"

Talking will help only if you listen to each other and do something positive about what you hear.

"How come I can repeat something over and over and he still doesn't understand?"

Because the misunderstanding's on a loop. Clarify what you mean by saying it another way.

"Is there an art to talking rather than squabbling?"

Yes. Take turns to talk, then recap and discuss what's been said.

"When we don't know the solution, should we decide on something anyway?"

Immediacy is rarely necessary, and the best answers often arrive following sleep and time.

"Sometimes I go quiet because I don't know what else to say. Why does this exasperate her so much?"

Because it seems like sulking. Give her a hug and explain that you're talked out for the moment and all will be well.

"Why does he get so annoyed when I tell him how I would do something he's doing?"

He feels as if you're pushing him to do it your way and not listening to his opinion or appreciating his own ability.

"Why does she ignore me when I tell her how to do things?"

You're coming across as a know-it-all. Even if you do know it all, it's often diplomatic to keep quiet unless you're asked to help.

"How come she usually makes me feel it's my fault?"

It's a common habit. Agree to stop blaming and shaming each other completely and for ever.

"When we try to talk, I can't get a word in. How can I make it fairer?"

Make an agreement to take turns and listen when the other's speaking, and keep to it, pointing it out if he forgets and takes over.

"How can we talk a lot when we're so busy we hardly see each other?"

Make time not just to communicate by talk but by being together, showing your love for each other and appreciating each other.

"Are relationships really worth giving time to?"

Yes. Giving time to your loved ones is the most important thing you can possibly do for them and for yourself.

"What's the minimum amount of time we should devote to talking?"

No matter how busy you are, each week set aside a couple of hours to chat or talk about what's going on in your lives.

"Will it matter if we don't communicate much?"

If you want your relationship to continue, yes it matters hugely.

"I have to work to make money. Surely it would be crazy to jeopardize that for love?"

Yes. But it also would be crazy to jeopardize love for money.

"I don't have much time to spend with my wife. Surely that's ok when she knows I love her?"

It's not ok at all because spending time with her is the best way to show her she matters to you.

"We want to have more time for each other, but how can we make more hours in the day?"

You can't, so stop trying to do it all and put your relationship at the top of your to-do list.

"Our sex life is great, but I miss talking about sex. How do we start?"

In bed, after some great lovemaking, let the intimacy flow through your thoughts into words.

"Is it good to talk about sex?"

Yes, it's great because it's an eternally interesting subject. You will learn about each other and it will deepen your intimacy.

"Is it good to talk while we're having sex?"

If you both like to talk, it's fine. Silence is fine too if one or both prefer it.

"Is there a way not to talk about sex?"

As ever, don't be accusatory, controlling or demeaning. As long as you think love, you'll be fine.

"I'm less articulate than she is, so how can I be confident enough when we want to talk about sex?"

Talk slowly, with mutual love and respect, and it will be fun finding the right words and understanding each other.

"How can we start talking about sex without embarrassment?"

Desensitize yourselves by reading a book about sexual techniques aloud to each other. Talking about sex gets easy surprisingly quickly.

"Should I say what's wrong with his sexual technique?"

Save words for praising what's good, and also show him through touch and your own lovemaking how to please you.

Lasting love

"We want our new relationship to be happy for ever. Is there a good way to start?"

Yes. Write down your definitions of a loving relationship. Remember that these are your aims, and they will help your love stay strong and sure.

"Does a good relationship take a lot of hard work?"

It takes care and maintenance, but that needn't be hard work.

"What if our life together isn't always good?"

Life and love are like a tapestry of feelings and experiences. Learn the art of seeing how the contrasts in tone and shade highlight the overall beauty.

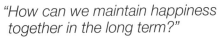

"How can we maintain happiness together in the long term?"

By paying attention to each other and your relationship and by adapting any changes so they benefit all three: you, your partner and your relationship.

"We're so busy we often go for days barely saying a word to each other. Does it matter if we don't talk much?"

Yes, because talking keeps you in touch with each other's thoughts and feelings.

"Physically, what's the best way to cheer each other up?"

Give each other a hug. It will make you both feel cherished, understood, safe and even healed.

"We'd like, one day, to be one of the couples you see in the papers who celebrate six or more decades of marriage. How do they last the course?"

They show up for one another every day, lovingly.

"How can we stay contented to be together?"

By keeping and relishing a feeling of belonging together.

"Is it so important to be nice to each other all the time?"

Yes, for although love will survive occasional grouchiness, to flourish it needs you both to behave lovingly most of the time.

"We love each other in our own way. Is it all right that our relationship isn't like that of our friends'?"

Yes. Every couple is unique, and it's great that you've found your own special form of harmony.

"I try to be nice to my partner most of the time, so why can't he put up with it when I'm not so affable?"

Love tolerates each other's down times, as long as you don't go for each other personally. If *not so affable* means unkind or horrid, think again and make an effort to change the way you behave towards your partner.

"Does the path of true love ever run smoothly?"

Yes, as long as you ski the ups and downs together.

"What's the best way to protect our love?"

Realizing how it would feel to lose it will help you cherish each other so that you don't.

"Isn't it tedious to explore your love and relationship and try to help it along?"

No. It's a fascinating, rewarding and fulfilling process.

"Could our ideals of love be too high?"

Yes. Remember that you are both human and make allowances for each other.

"Does is matter that we've been together for so long we've started to take each other for granted?"

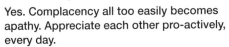

Yes. Complacency all too easily becomes apathy. Appreciate each other pro-actively, every day.

"Is it all right to shout at my partner if she breaks something?"

No. It will cause hurt and hostility, and her feelings are far more important than any material object.

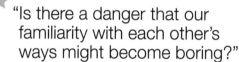

"Is there a danger that our familiarity with each other's ways might become boring?"

Keep surprising each other now and then (nicely, that is!) and remember to pay attention to each other too, and you'll always be interested in each other.

"I often do things, like booking a weekend break, on the spur of the moment without consulting my partner. How can I stop my impulsive nature causing problems between us?"

Before acting on impulse, think if what you are going to do might irritate or otherwise adversely affect your partner. If the answer's yes, hold back.

"How can we continue to treasure our love forever?"

Take responsibility for it every day and cherish it as if it were a precious treasure, for it is the most precious treasure there is.

"I love the familiarity that's growing between us, but will we start to neglect each other?"

No, not as long as you remember not to. Every day appreciate each other and the wonderful intimacy you share, and you won't take it for granted.

"What if I don't sympathize with my partner about something?"

Be compassionate anyway, because it will help you to develop understanding.

"A mutual friend told us we need to lighten up because we take our love so seriously. Should we try to change?"

Love is important and needs taking care of, but enjoy it and have lots of fun, too.

"What if my partner and I mature at different rates and grow apart?"

Be aware of the progress you're both making and keep talking about it, and you'll stay side by side in your relationship.

"We've been happy for many years, and I worry it can't last much longer. Is there anything I can do to protect our love?"

Yes. Chase fear away by enjoying your happiness and continuing to love and care for each other.

"We love each other, but whenever we have a dispute we end up having furious rows. Is there a better way?"

Fighting and arguing won't solve your differences. Listening, understanding and warm hearts eager to resolve the issues will.

"I love my partner and want to make it work, but will I have the perseverance?"

Summon it at all costs, because if it is to last a happy relationship takes time and energy as well as love.

"Surely love can be spontaneous?"

Yes, love often exists completely spontaneously. But we can do a lot to help our feelings of love happen and endure.

"How can we stay close when we both have very active, busy lives?"

By underpinning your lives with mutual tenderness and intimacy.

"How much time do we need to spend together?"

Enough time to stay connected, enjoy each other's company and make love.

"Am I silly to be scared of losing all the benefits of my single life?"

No, it's sensible to think things through. Remember, though, that you will be pooling resources and will both benefit hugely from the joy of living together lovingly.

"Sometimes we fool around like children. Is this immature?"

No, it's wonderful. Being playful adds zest to love all through our lives.

"He brings his work problems home, and I try to help him resolve them. How can I avoid getting as stressed by them as he is?"

Make a consciously decision not to take the stress of his problems on board. If you're calm and positive you will help him relax too.

"She would like to be with me every minute. Is it wrong of me to want time alone or to be with friends independently of her?"

No. Most of us need some individual time apart, and it will give your relationship air to breathe.

"We'd love to stay in love for ever, but do we have a choice in the matter?"

You always have a choice to love each other and to get on well together every single day. Keep making the decision to do so and your love will thrive.

"I put more into our relationship than he does. Am I loving him too much?"

No, for being loving and generous is a great joy. And in other phases of life he may put more in than you so go with the flow of love's tide.

"Is love something we can create?"

Often, yes, given enough compatibility and mutual enthusiasm.

"After many years together, can we recapture the joy of the early days together?"

Yes. Make an effort to remember and re-create past magic moments as well as being alert to new spontaneous ones.

"We used to feel so deeply connected and in love when we gazed up at the sky at night. How have we lost that magic?"

The stars and the moon are still there. So is your love. Go and look for them, often. Enjoy.

"Does it matter that we each grab our own breakfast before dashing off to work?"

Not if it suits you. Make up for lost time together by enjoying leisurely breakfasts together at weekends and when you're on holiday.

"What's your best advice for keeping romance alive?"

Always retain a sense of wonder that your love is so good and that you are both so lucky.

"I miss romantic, sexy breakfasts in bed but she doesn't because she can't stand crumbs on the sheets. How can I change her mind?"

Promise to make the bed with clean sheets when you get up; and make sure you do!

"Why do we feel so romantic when we eat outside on holiday?"

The air, the ambience, the fact that you are relaxed. Take time to eat together outside or by a window at home and re-create those loving feelings.

"Is being tactile important to romance?"

Yes, because even the briefest touch transmits your love in an instant and can still make you both glow with pleasure.

"We still adore each other after 60 years. Does it matter that he's the most unromantic man on earth?"

Not a bit, because your relationship sounds as romantic as they come, whatever his personal take on romance!

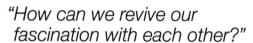

"How can we revive our fascination with each other?"

Take a keen, active, ongoing interest in each other's thoughts and ideas, and make an effort to be interesting.

"Sometimes my partner's opinions, about religion, for instance, are based on muddled reasoning. Should I keep quiet?"

No. It's great to challenge each other's thinking in a loving, supportive atmosphere. But first listen carefully and repeat what you think he's said to make sure you've got it right.

"Should I empathize with and adopt my partner's mood, or should I try to lift him out of it?"

Each situation is different, so respond intuitively with love in your heart.

"Should I try to keep calm to counteract my girlfriend's up and down personality?"

It could feel restrictive to you and manipulative to her. Be your natural self and free your relationship to find its own unique balance.

"Will my partner's new ideas about philosophy make us grow apart?"

No. Help each other mature in your own individual ways with tender, understanding support and your love will flourish in tandem.

"Will we get too set in our ways now that we're planning to stay together for ever?"

You'll always be alert and interesting if you inspire each other to think freshly and stay passionate about life and love.

"What should I do if my partner cannot sleep because of stress?"

Showing that you love and feel for him with a hug, a cup of tea or a shoulder massage will make him feel worlds better.

"My partner's self-confidence suffered when we realized that we're getting old. How can I put the spring back in her step?"

Tell her that you love her as much as ever and always will. Be romantic. Look at her and touch her as though she's gorgeous.

"My partner knows I love him, so why should I show it more often?"

Because showing your love in words or actions will keep his belief in your love strong.

"Although we love each other, we never show or think about it. Should we?"

Definitely. Feelings have little point if they're ignored. Enjoy your love positively while you can, as it's a huge blessing.

"What should I do when the way my partner behaves irritates me?"

Release your frustration safely by telling him how you're feeling about what he has done rather than accusing or nagging him. He's more likely change the way he acts if you do this, and he won't feel so hurt.

"When our marriage goes through a rocky patch why does my partner get so anxious?"

She's scared. Tell her that you love her and reassure her that together you'll resolve what's wrong.

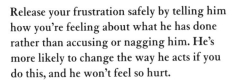

"Now we're thinking of splitting up we look back and see how happy we could have been. Why didn't we appreciate it at the time?"

Because you ignored it, just as you are doing now. Notice the love that's still between you, cherish it and enjoy it to the full, today and every day you have left.

"Why are relationships so complicated?"

Because we're complex emotional, sensitive creatures with a tendency to think too much, or not enough, about relationships and love.

"Should I tell my partner I can't live without him in order to keep him with me?"

No, because need constricts and impersonates love. True love cherishes but trusts, sets free but provides a haven of love and security.

"How can we simplify our relationship so that we can enjoy the love between us?"

Forget about the present and future and deal with the present positively, caringly and as simply as possible.

"Does feeling the emotion of love become easier if you concentrate on feeling loving more often?"

Yes, like most things, the more we work at love, the better we get at it.

"Sometimes we squabble. Is it because we're too close?"

Being close is fine, but remember that you are not children arguing but mature people who have chosen to live together and love each other, and act like it.

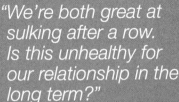

"We're both great at sulking after a row. Is this unhealthy for our relationship in the long term?"

Yes. Cut out the sulking and get on with enjoying life together while you can. Don't waste a moment!

"My partner's comments are always constructive, so how can I stop myself feeling undermined?"

See any advice as an opportunity for thought, and, if it's apt, act on it. If not, tell him it's unjustified and have him rethink.

"Why doesn't she like it when I'm apologetic?"

Perhaps too frequent apologies seem weak or false to her. Alternatively, she might find it difficult to admit that she's wrong herself. Talk about it.

"Is there any hope for what seems like a loveless relationship?"

Yes. If the two of you want and are prepared to be loving and lovable, you can between you create love.

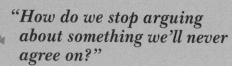

"How do we stop arguing about something we'll never agree on?"

Say something like, *Interesting discussion, let's agree to differ*. Love is big enough for a lot of differences.

" I hate rows and try to avoid disagreeing with my partner. But I have to be honest about my thoughts, don't I?"

Yes, it's healthy to have your own viewpoints. Emotion is fine too, but don't be nasty to each other.

"My partner says I'm arrogant. Why doesn't she appreciate my success?"

It sounds as if your pride is making you appear pompous or intolerant. Try to be a bit humble, and let your kind and loving side shine out.

"We talk a lot about our relationship. Why don't we ever seem to solve anything?"

You need to listen more to each other's point of view and to resolve any issues as a team.

"How can we stop everyday stresses and worries spoiling our happiness together?"

By stopping worrying. Do anything that needs to be done, then think and enjoy the bright side of life.

"How can I remind myself that I love her when we're going through a bad patch?"

When you're getting on well, write down all the things you love about each other. Next time you're hostile, get out the list, laugh and make up.

"How can I make him realize I can't be perfect?"

Have a chat about the impossibility of perfection and the need to accept each other as you are.

"She thinks I'm perfect. Is it ok to be put on a pedestal?"

No, you can only fall off. It would be better for her to know and love you as you really are, flaws and all.

"Do we have to put our all into our relationship, all the time?"

Nothing as exhausting as that! Plenty of love and attention most of the time will be fine.

"Our love is like a roller-coaster. Would we be better off finding partners with whom we'd have a less fiery life?"

You're relationship has many pluses and a lot of love, so stick with it. Encourage more ups than downs by talking instead of rowing, and enjoy the middle ground in between.

"Even when we've made up after a disagreement, I'll keep replaying who said what. How can I let it go?"

By telling yourself firmly, *Forget it now*.

"Sometimes I get annoyed with my partner because I feel so irritated, even though she's done nothing."

It sounds as if your irritation is coming from another area, such as your work or personal issues. Remember that your partner is your ally and love her.

"I've been horrible to my partner for no good reason. How can I make up to her for all I've said and done?"

By apologizing wholeheartedly and by behaving lovingly and caringly from now on.

"Isn't compromising the same as doing a U-turn?"

No. In relationships compromise is usually the loving, diplomatic way to resolve things.

"At work I have to be strong and unwavering. What's the best way to be at home: confident leader or new man?"

You can be both if you're flexible and take turns with your partner to make decisions and lead.

"I find it difficult to forgive him even when he's said sorry. How can I stop myself replaying what he did?"

Concentrate on loving him and enjoying his company and you won't have the time or inclination to brood.

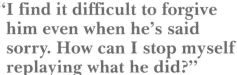

"I seethe with anger when we fight, but surely it's good to express our negative emotions?"

It's good to be aware of them, yes, but talk the issues through logically and fairly when you both feel calmer.

*"When we argue the anger and
pain stay with me for days. Is
my reaction normal?"*

It's quite common, yes, but it doesn't have to be
normal for you! Resolve anything wrong between
you and then dismiss lingering negative feelings
from your mind.

"When we've had a row we sleep in separate rooms. Is this a good idea?"

*No. Always say you're sorry to each other
before you go to sleep, and then have a
cuddle or curl up together like spoons.*

*"Is there any hope for our
relationship when there are so
many things wrong with it?"*

There's every hope, for every time you make an
improvement, no matter how small, your whole
relationship will improve.

"My partner says I never back him up when we're talking with friends. If I don't think he's right, should I lie?"

No, but nor should you play devil's advocate. When you agree with him, say so and always defend to the hilt his right to his own view.

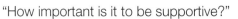

"How important is it to be supportive?"

Being a rock of support is one of the most wonderful things we can do for each other.

"Is there anything we can do to promote love when we're apart?"

Anticipate the happiness of seeing each other again and feel it flow through you now.

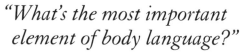

"What's the most important element of body language?"

Make eye contact often. Looking into each other's eyes helps to forge a strong mind-body-soul connection.

"Can you recommend a good therapeutic gift?"

Yes. Take turns to give each other a non-sexual massage. There's nothing like it for making you feel loving and loved.

"I love her but often find myself being gruff in the evening after work. How can I change this?"

On the way home decide to be good-tempered all evening and visualize the companionability that results.

"How can I physically express my love for my partner without necessarily touching him?"

Turn towards him. Your heart will go out to him and he'll bask in the warmth of your love.

"Is there an easy and effective way to brighten each other up?"

Yes. Smile and laugh together.

"Would relaxing together be good for our marriage?"

Yes it would. The combination of relaxation, pleasure and intimacy is love's soul food.

"No matter which evening class course I start, my partner wants to do it too. Most of the time I'm pleased to have him along with me, but would it be selfish to say occasionally that I'd like to take up something on my own?"

No. It's good to have at least one individual interest. Next time you intend enrolling for a new course, tell him you love studying with him usually but this time you'd like to do this particular one on your own.

"How can I help her go to sleep at night?"

Lie together like spoons and breathe in the same rhythm as she does: it's as soothing as a lullaby.

"Is it best for one of us to do the cooking, to take turns or to share?"

Whichever you're both happy with. The important thing is to relax and enjoy preparing food together so that you can fully enjoy sharing your meal.

"How can we show we still enjoy being together as much as ever?"

Apart from the main things you do together, seek out each other's company for a few minutes now and then for no particular reason.

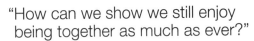

"Without appearing schmaltzy, how can I tell my wife how much she means to me?"

You could read her a poem that expresses your joy in her. Give her a compliment with pleasure and love glowing in your eyes. Or simply say, Thank goodness we met. I love you.

Trust

LOVE

"What is trust?"

In a relationship trust is the confidence that your partner is reliable and loving.

"I know that my partner is always there for me if I need him. Is this a form of trust?"

Yes, it's a wonderful one.

"Is it usually better to be trusting?"

Yes, because your belief strengthens you and those you believe in.

"If I trust my partner too soon, will I scare him off?"

Trust is part of love and draws people to you. Distrust pushes love away.

"If I let go of fear and trust my partner, will there be an immediate result?"

Yes, a lovely one. You'll find you can have fun and play together much more easily.

"Will I trust myself better if my partner trusts me?"

Yes. Trust bonds and deepens when we trust each other.

"I love my partner but don't know if I have the courage to trust her. What should I do?"

It takes courage to love, so harness your courage to trust. They go side by side.

"Is it safe to be open and frank with each other?"

Yes, but remember to be kind and sensitive in your openness and in the way you respond.

"Her trust frightens me. Am I good enough for it?"

 Yes, if you want to be, because recognizing the importance of her trust is the first step to valuing and guarding it.

"My partner wants to be faithful from now on. Is it worth making the huge effort it will take to trust him?"

Absolutely, because the harder it is to trust, the greater the peace will be when you do and the greater the joy you will experience when your partner lives up to your trust.

"Is it sensible to be suspicious?"

Aware, yes, suspicious no. Suspicion strangles love; trust gives love free rein.

"Should we love each other more than we love ourselves?"

Not necessarily, and although often we might put our loved ones first, it's important to love and value ourselves highly too.

"How can I trust my fiancé to let me be myself?"

Agree with him that the love and intimacy you share will support your personal growth and expression and will never restrict your potential.

"How can I trust my fiancé not to exploit me financially if we ever get divorced?"

Try to gauge his integrity and honesty and then see if he is willing to enter into a pre-nuptial agreement. That done, remember that love and trust are usually well worth the leap of faith they need to flourish.

"How can I not doubt my previously errant partner now that he's promised to be faithful?"

Don't look backwards or worry about the future. Live in the light of his pledge today.

"I feel so guilty that I weakly betrayed my partner. How can I make it up to her?"

Learn from your mistake, and be aware of temptation and steadfastly ignore it.

"What will happen if I let my partner down?"

Being uncertain of your ability to be strong will help you be courageous in guarding against your weakness.

"Why is someone's complete trust so scary?"

Because mutual trust means a soul connection.

"I often annoy my partner by changing my plans at the last minute without telling her. Can you recommend a way to help me be more dependable?"

Yes. Remember to tread carefully, considering her feelings, for if you are careless you will trample her love for you under your feet.

"Why is it important to trust each other?"

Trust makes it possible to enjoy feelings of security and relaxation and elbows out suspicion and bitterness.

*"Will trust encourage my partner
to be strong and keep her word?"*

Yes. Your trust will give your partner confidence
that she is trustworthy and encourage her to be so.

"Are some people more likely to be trustworthy than others?"

Yes. People who had the example of dependable
parents or other carers are more likely to be
trustworthy themselves. But anyone can learn or
choose to be trustworthy at any stage of their life.

"My new boyfriend seems genuine, but even so trusting him will be a huge step for me. Do I take it?"

Yes. Don't be afraid to take a big step if you love each other and it feels right.

"What is the chief ingredient of trust?"

Mutually caring, respectful conduct.

"Will I naturally become more trusting as I get older?"

Not necessarily. Trusting a partner, like loving them, doesn't necessarily happen naturally and is a decision we need to make every day.

"Is it all right to play around while I'm young?"

It's never all right to deliberately mislead or let people down. Avoid making commitments or giving an impression you don't mean.

"My boyfriend doesn't trust anyone. Will he ever be able to trust me?"

Yes. With courage he can in time learn from your example of reliability and steadfast love to trust in you.

"If I don't believe in my own reliability, how can I trust my partner?"

You have the ability, so be courageous and be reliable. Then you will know that others can be reliable too.

"Can we speed up the development of trust between us?"

Yes, by reliably being good, loyal friends.

"If I trust her, might she still betray me?"

Perhaps. But love is trusting in the moment and does not worry about the future.

"What does trust mean in a loving relationship?"

It means accepting each other as you really are and expecting loving actions and support.

"How can I trust him when so many couples break up because of infidelity?"

For inspiration remember the millions of people who are worthy of trust and the many, many happy relationships there are in the world.

"Is it fair to expect to live up to each other's trust when all humans are so fallible?"

Trust is believing that you won't let each other down even though you accept each other's fallibility and don't expect perfection.

"I know I am trustworthy, but how do I know he is?"

Because you are trustworthy, you know he can be too.

"Can anyone be trustworthy?"

Yes. We are all capable of making the decision to be trustworthy and sticking by our resolution.

"How can I tell whether she will be faithful?"

As you get to know each other, you will sense the depth of her intention and strength.

"I've been hurt so many times before, how can I believe my new partner will be honourable?"

Faith in him will come, if you allow it to, as he proves to you over time that he's dependable.

"My boyfriend sometimes flirts outrageously and I worry he'll be unfaithful one day. I try to trust him, but how can I discourage his abuse of my trust?"

By challenging any actions, including lascivious flirting, that reveal carelessness about your feelings.

"Surely blind trust is foolish?"

Yes. Lovingly trusting someone doesn't mean that you should bury your head in the sand if your partner treats you inconsiderately.

"*I trust my partner completely, but how can I learn to relax when other men are talking to her?*"

Remind yourself of your confidence in her fidelity to you and decide to relax. It's the only way to oust suspicion.

"How can I fully trust my partner if I'm constantly on the alert for betrayal?"

Being alert isn't the same as worrying or being suspicious. If you pay attention to each other you will naturally pick up on any problems.

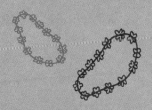

"I will never let my partner down, but how can I help her believe in me?"

Show your love every day and reaffirm your commitment to her often. And don't flirt with other people or otherwise give cause for jealousy.

"Is there a remedy for our distrust of trust?"

Yes, love. Although we can all make mistakes, love strengthens us and our relationships and helps us mend any accidental damage we do.

"Although I used to be promiscuous, I would never let my partner down. How can I convince her that she can trust me?"

With constant reassurance, and living up to it.

"How can I trust my partner not to judge me if I tell him the truth about me?"

Affirm to each other that you will do your best to understand whatever you tell each other and will continue to respect and stand by each other.

"I've pretended to be the kind of woman I knew my boyfriend wanted. Should I continue to live the lie?"

No. Love of a mirage is worthless.

"Should I always tell my partner if there's something about him I don't like?"

No. Part of the art and kindness of love is knowing when to overlook things.

"Is it fair of my partner to nag me about things I can't change?"

No it's not. It's loving and wise to accept things that can't be changed.

"How can I tell him who I really am?"

Be brave and give him the chance to love the real you.

"Is it honest to promise my new partner that I'll be faithful when I wasn't to my ex-wife?"

Yes. If you are aware of your fallibility, you can resolve to resist temptation and keep your promise this time.

"We'd like to marry and pledge fidelity to each other, but we're worried we won't always feel the same. Is there a way we can authentically get married anyway?"

Instead of the traditional wording, you could promise each other that you will forsake all others while you love each other and wish to be together.

"My partner's nervous about whether she can be faithful to someone for the rest of her life. Commitment is vital to me, so should we break it off now?"

Give her time. She may realize that she can be faithful to you and that you're not just someone.

"Is it normal to be nervous of the marriage promises?"

Yes, but love and trust in yourselves will overcome your fear.

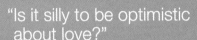

"Is it silly to be optimistic about love?"

It's very sensible, because optimism encourages love to thrive.

"How can I believe that there's still love in our relationship?"

By being loving and encouraging your partner to be loving too.

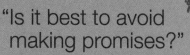

"Is it best to avoid making promises?"

Promises you mean to keep and know you can are fine, but don't make promises that you're unlikely to keep.

"Does it matter if we don't keep promises?"

Yes, because promises kept inspire trust.

"What if I can't do something I've promised?"

Keep your partner informed and it will lessen disappointment and save him from thinking badly of you.

"When my new girlfriend says, *I love you*, can I take it to be true?"

It depends on many things, so for now enjoy the declaration but don't read a lot into it until you know what she really means by the words.

"She said she loved me but broke up with me soon afterwards. How can I trust anyone who says, *I love you* again?"

Trust that they mean it in the moment and be glad.

"When my boyfriend says he will always love me, should I believe he always will?"

Only trust that love will be long lasting if your whole relationship with each other indicates over time that this is the case.

"Should I be patient if my partner lets me down?"

Yes, if it's the first time or a very occasional happening. Otherwise, talk about the need for reliability and trust in a loving relationship.

"I'm concerned that my boyfriend's love didn't last long in his previous marriages. Should I marry him even so?"

Only if he can convince you that, this time, he is determined to be steadfast.

"My partner's untrustworthy, but we love each other. Am I foolish to stay with her?"

There's great hope for your relationship if she's determined to become trustworthy and if you support her as she learns new habits.

"My partner says I should be glad that he's trustworthy most of the time, but shouldn't he always be?"

Yes. Dependability is a fixture in a good relationship and trust can't live without it.

"I've no reason to be jealous, so why am I?"

Look at what your fear is showing: that you're insecure in yourself. Start developing a sense of inner security that will let you enjoy mutual love and trust.

"Does my jealous nature rule out trust no matter how much we love each other?"

No, don't let jealousy rule you. Deal with it effectively by building your self-respect and your belief in your partner's ability to be true.

"When I get fearful, how can I stop irrational jealousy creeping in?"

By using logic to rationalize fears.

"Surely I'm right to be jealous when he's unfaithful?"

Your jealousy is understandable, but that doesn't mean it's helpful. You both need to look at and address the reasons for his infidelity and restrengthen your bond.

"How can I be brave enough to give my heart?"

Loving is a leap of faith. But no matter what happens, love is never wasted. So be courageous. Take the leap.

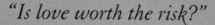

"Is love worth the risk?"

Yes, for although we take a risk and may be hurt when we love, we always reap joy.

"How can we trust our love when relationships can change?"

By trusting that you will do your best to adapt to change and new direction both willingly and lovingly.

"How do I stop being afraid that I might change?"

Trust yourself to be loving and dependable as you develop.

"My partner is scared I'll leave her. How can I make her see I won't?"

With time, patience and love. Encourage her self-esteem so she is less dependent and can trust without fear.

"Is there a way we can help ourselves to be faithful and true?"

Imagine yourselves as a steadfastly loving, supportive couple and walk together on the path towards your goal.

"Does trust just happen?"

It may appear to, but actually trust is a very active quality. You both need to be trustworthy, and you both need to trust.

"Isn't it better to play safe and withhold trust?"

Only if you've clear reason to feel it's not merited. Otherwise, trust in trust because it feels good and encourages others to be trustworthy.

"My partner finds it difficult to trust me. I know I won't let him down so does his distrust matter?"

Yes, because it's an unpleasant feeling that could cause or contribute to problems between you. Help him build his self-esteem and his regard for you.

"Am I responsible for my partner's trust in me?"

Yes. It's in your hands, and you have the ability to keep it safe.

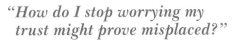

"How do I stop worrying my trust might prove misplaced?"

Trust in your love, day by day, knowing that whatever happens you will cope.

"When relationships are often fraught and short lived, how can we trust in love at all?"

By thinking of the most loving way to handle any situation that might arise. Doing this will help light up the path ahead and may resolve relationship problems too.

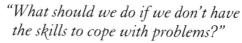

"What should we do if we don't have the skills to cope with problems?"

Trust that your relationship is a learning curve, and with love and sensitivity you'll come through just fine.

"What's the point of another relationship when two divorces have proved to me it may not last?"

When you and a loved one enjoy and choose to be together, the union is a time of tenderness and joy. Trust in its beauty and cherish the love you share.

"Isn't trust foolish when anyone may or may not be faithful?"

No, trust is sensible for it's love and life and hope affirming and always feels a thousand times better than distrust.

"I've always trusted my partners. Because one let me down, should I be more suspicious of my new partner?"

No, do trust him. Trust feels good, and as long as you chose him carefully and want to be faithful to each other, suspicion is unfounded.

"How can we rebuild our marriage after a much regretted affair?"

By delighting in the relief you want to be together, the contentment of being together and the satisfaction of doing it better than ever.

"How much should I trust my partner?"

Trust, like love, isn't something you need to ration. Once you let it flow it constantly replenishes and grows.

"How should I deal with my partner's knack of putting doubts into my head?"

Get him to look at his defeatist habit. Once he's aware of it he can try encouraging your positivity with his own.

"How can I make myself trust him?"

There's only one way: only you can decide to be trusting. It's usually a huge relief.

"Won't I kick myself if I trust my partner and she betrays me again?"

Distrust is uncomfortable and wouldn't lessen the hurt of a further betrayal, so you've nothing to lose by being trusting.

"What do I stand to gain if I trust him?"

You'll reap the rewards of relaxed happiness and he will be more likely to try to be deserving of your trust.

Sex & wellbeing

"Is it best when sex is associated with love?"

It's wonderful when the two are linked, for sure, but love can be good without sex and vice versa. Together, though, they're a match made in heaven.

"What's better about loving sex than any great sex?"

The pleasure of casual sex is short lived, but feel-good factor of loving sex lingers long afterwards and deepens love.

"What does loving sex do for a relationship?"

It gives an ongoing feeling of intimacy and makes it easier to get on well generally.

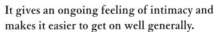

THE JOY OF SEX   307

"How can I prevent old, negative feelings about sex affecting our sex life now we're permanently together?"

Love in the moment and be glad for your sexuality and your enjoyment of sex with your partner.

"Are love and sex good for us?"

Love is an emotional and physical tonic and so is loving sex. Together they put us on Cloud Nine.

"Do we need to feel good about our sexuality to have good sex?"

Feeling good about your sexuality will give it the opportunity to flourish and enrich your relationship. It's an ongoing process.

"How important is sex in a loving relationship?"

It depends on the couple, but it is important that both partners are happy about the quantity and quality of their lovemaking.

"Is sex different when you love your partner?"

Yes, loving your partner adds another dimension of pleasure.

"Sex is fantastic on holiday, but back at home desire wanes. How can we get that holiday feeling?"

Think of the things that turn you on: warmth, swimming, romantic music and, most of all, taking time to be together, and enjoy them at home too.

"Can I get back that feeling I had early in our relationship when I wanted my partner so much?"

Yes. Recall those erotic times that completely aroused you and led to brilliant lovemaking.

"We want lots more honeymoons, but can't take the sun and heat. Any ideas?"

Pick a trip that makes you both go Wow, that sounds brilliant. A seaside break? A course? An activity break? Go for it!

"Do men and women have different takes on sex?"

Attitudes have evened up, but men still tend to be more casual about sex than women.

"The stereotype on television is that women in long-term relationships want sex much less than men. Is this always true?"

No, many women have as high a sex drive as their partners.

"Why does it make me feel used when my partner suddenly pounces on me out of the blue?"

It's because like most women you like to be seduced by a slow build-up of loving attention.

"How do I tell my partner that I don't want quickie sex out of the blue?"

Tell him that when he climaxes fast after jumping straight in it neither arouses nor satisfies you.

"Why doesn't my partner realize that women usually take more time than men to get aroused and have an orgasm?"

Because, sadly, so many women fake it.

"Is it ok to fake an orgasm when I'm tired?"

No. It will create a false expectation in your partner. Just say, *It's been lovely but I'm not going to have an orgasm.* We don't have to climax every time.

"Do women, in general, need more persuasion than men to have sex, and, if so, why?"

Yes, because their sex drive is, generally, more influenced by hormone levels, emotions and how well they are getting on with their partner.

"In film and television dramas the characters are always up for sex and climax almost instantly. Is it ok to be content with once or twice a month and to take our time?"

Drama is illusion. Your love life is wonderful. Enjoy it.

"How often is normal?"

The average is supposed to be two or three times a week, but who knows for real, because people often exaggerate in surveys about sex.

"Ought we to aim for the so-called average?"

What other people are or aren't doing is irrelevant. What matters is that you are both content with your lovemaking.

"We don't make love any more because of relationship, not sexual problems. Should we see a relationship advisor or a sex therapist?"

Relationship problems tend to cause sexual problems and vice versa. It would be a good idea to see a psychosexual therapist.

"My new girlfriend is anxious about sex. How can I help?"

Enjoy affectionate and sensual touching in a non-sexual way until she is ready to lead or follow you forward sexually. Therapy could also be helpful for her.

"We love each other and want to make love but are finding intercourse difficult. Would psychosexual therapy help?"

Yes. The therapist will advise you on ways to get together comfortably.

"Which is more important in lovemaking, love or experience?"

Love gives tenderness and intimacy; experience may increase sensuality and comfort and make climax easier. Both are good.

"What's the most important quality of lovemaking?"

To care as much about giving pleasure as enjoying it yourself.

"Be honest: does size matter?"

Only if you are prejudiced about size, but not a jot if you're mutually attracted and enthusiastic to find out how you can enjoy great sex together.

"Do our brains have anything to do with love and sex?"

Yes. Every aspect of our lives is recorded by the brain and to a great extent controlled by it.

"Do different areas of the brain look after different zones of love and sex?"

The limbic zone monitors sexual habits, feelings and pleasure. Genital stimulation and sexual reactions and hormonal output are controlled by the hypothalamus, and the cerebrum organizes our sexual thoughts and wishes.

"Can thinking about love and sexual desire and pleasure trigger or increase them?"

Absolutely. Even with no sensual input, thought can fire the physiological links.

"Can we climax just by thinking about it?"

Yes. It's perfectly possible, just as erotic dreams can culminate in orgasm.

"How does love affect the process of sex?"

It encourages you to give and receive pleasure and increases the flow of feel-good hormones.

"Why do we feel so sexy when we're in the early days of a relationship?"

The chemicals that cause and are released by early intense attraction hot up our sex drive.

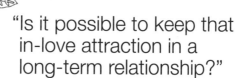

"Is it possible to keep that in-love attraction in a long-term relationship?"

You can encourage it by recalling how you felt in the early stages of your relationship or by fantasizing about sexy scenes or books with your partner as the hero.

"Does eating together increase the aphrodisiacal effect of food?"

Yes. Sharing a meal can be a sensual and intimate pleasure, which will turn you both on.

"My partner's tired of the way I turn away from him when he wants sex. How can I save our marriage?"

Turn towards him. Connect, emotionally and physically, and enjoy the feel of your bodies and minds touching. Love him.

 "If he won't make love, is it because of a problem in our relationship?"

Not necessarily. Stress, ill health or tiredness can sabotage desire. If it keeps happening, talk about it.

"What's your best advice for great sex in a long-term relationship?"

Accept that great sex won't generally be spontaneous, so plan ahead and make a special time for it.

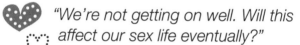

"We're not getting on well. Will this affect our sex life eventually?"

Yes, because a good relationship enhances sex. So face what's wrong together and get your love back on track.

"We both enjoy making love once we get going, so why am I so often reluctant?"

Perhaps your sex drive isn't pushing you or you're suppressing it. Think through your reluctance to its cause, and you'll see how to spark desire more often.

"Will a problem with sex endanger our love?"

Yes it could, if one or both of you miss the shared pleasure and intimacy of good sex. Resolve what's wrong, seeking expert help if necessary.

"Does it matter how we make love?"

Yes. It matters very much that it's pleasurable for both of you.

"When we're having sex, how can I stop the worry I'm not much good at it?"

Stop thinking about your expertise or the lack of it and start enjoying giving and appreciating wonderful sensations.

"Should I do the things my partner wants to do but that I'm uncomfortable with?"

If you don't like something, or the idea of it, don't do it. Loving sex is about mutual pleasure and is never coerced.

"Do we need lots of time?"

Normally as much as is sufficient for your arousal to rise in tandem and for you both to climax, which is usually around 10 to 20 minutes.

"Quickie sex can be satisfying, can't it?"

In fun terms yes it can, but aside from the early days of passion, most women rarely climax that quickly. For them and for men, too, once they're used to the pleasure of it, a slower arousal curve is usually best.

"What if he comes too quickly?"

He could learn a technique to slow him down. Alternatively, concentrate on your pleasure first and climax, then it won't matter if, when it's his turn, he comes fast.

"Is it important to have a wide repertoire of lovemaking tactics?"

Not if you're both well satisfied with a few. But pushing your boundaries could be exciting and increase your enjoyment.

"How can I ease the boredom of being able to anticipate my partner's every move?"

Start taking the lead sometimes and guide him to new ways to please you and be pleased.

"How can I ease my boredom with something my girlfriend especially likes?"

Slip into a fantasy so that you stay turned on mentally as well as physically within a reasonable time limit.

"If we're taking turns to give each other pleasure I'll go on for ages, but he only returns the favour for a minute or two. Is this fair?"

No. Loving sex has a reasonably equal balance.

"Do we need to read books or watch videos on technique?"

Books and videos will speed up your acquisition of knowledge, but they aren't essential if you're intuitive, imaginative and like working at it!

"Does good sex always involve complicated or athletic moves?"

No. The simplest way you both love to make love can be stunningly good.

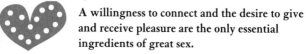

"How can I make up for not being able to move like a gymnast in bed any more?"

A willingness to connect and the desire to give and receive pleasure are the only essential ingredients of great sex.

"As we make love reasonably often but less than the average couple, should I squash the persistent feeling I'm missing out?"

Dissatisfaction will disappear if you remind yourself that good lovemaking is about quality and intimacy, not quantity.

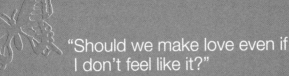

"Should we make love even if I don't feel like it?"

If you are willing, knowing you'll enjoy it once you get going, it's fine to make love. But if you feel pressured to or don't enjoy it, you both need to address the reasons.

"Is it ok to say no to sex?"

Yes, it's fine, now and then. If you keep avoiding sex, however, or are never enthusiastic about it, think about why you feel this way and do something about it.

"Her sex drive is lower than mine. Does it matter?"

Not at all if you're both prepared to compromise and make love a little more or less often than you'd respectively choose.

"She'd like to make love every night, but I'm a once-a-week man. How do we resolve this?"

Compromise and make love two or three times a week.

"How can I tell my partner that I'd love to share physical affection even though I've agreed to give up sex?"

Explain your need for loving contact and assure her that you won't see it as a prelude to sex so she can relax and enjoy it too.

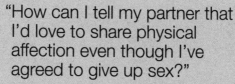

"Is it important to have similar sex drives?"

As long as you agree roughly how often you'll make love willingly, and enthusiasm are more important than matching libido.

"How can she possibly prefer reading to making love?"

Reading is personally undemanding. Sex takes lots of input and energy. Remind her of the pleasure, joy and intimacy that sex offers.

"Am I right to feel he doesn't love me when he won't make love?"

His lack of desire may have nothing to do with love or attraction. Agree how often you'd both be happy to make love.

"Which is the sexiest sense?"

All five are! But perhaps touch has the edge
because it feels so wonderful and offers so
much scope for variety.

"Is touch important?"

Very. Touching affirms your love, soothes
and, of course, it feels lovely to be touched
as well as to touch.

"Is music the food of love and, if so, why?"

*Yes, it can be because it makes us more aware of
our emotions and heightens them.*

"What's the most loving
physical thing we can do in
a non-sexual way?"

*Sensually massage or caress each other's skin
wherever the one being massaged asks: feet or
shoulders, for example.*

"*How do I get used
to being tactile?*"

Touch each other often and revel
in how it feels to be tactile
with each other.

"*Why does it affect me emotionally
as well as sexually when my
partner touches me?*"

Touch re-creates feelings of childhood when
our parents held us safely. In addition, touch
sends neurological signals to the brain,
releasing feel-good chemicals in response.

"Can touch communicate desire and love?"

Yes, erotically and emotionally the subtlest of touches can speak volumes.

"How should I touch my partner?"

With love in your hands.

"What sort of pressure should I use for caressing?"

Gentle but positive.

"What's the best technique for touching?"

Several feel fantastic: pulsing, pressing, stroking, caressing are all great.

"What are the most erogenous zones?"

Any part of the body can be. Ask your partner which his are.

"Should we hold back from explicit sexual touch early in our lovemaking?"

Building arousal slowly heightens pleasure and satisfaction. But sometime it's fun to move fast!

"After sex, is it fair that he goes straight to sleep?"

It's often natural. Snuggle into his arms or lie like spoons as he drifts off and you can still enjoy the bliss of post-lovemaking touch.

"Is there any way I shouldn't touch?"

Yes, don't be rough, and never, ever rub.

"Is it good to touch each other, aside from when we're having sex?"

Yes, we've an innate need to touch and be touched, both of which make us feel comfortable and peaceful.

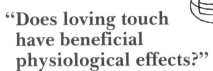

"Does loving touch have beneficial physiological effects?"

Yes, the haemoglobin in the blood increases, carrying oxygen to all the organs and aiding and healing us physically and emotionally.

"Should we keep the light on when we make love?"

Often, yes, because seeing your bodies, the way you move together and the expression of pleasure in your eyes can be a major turn-on.

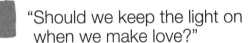

"Why do we love to gaze into each other's eyes?"

It's a sign that you're there for each other, and your eyes are windows into each other's soul.

"What are the most attractive facial expressions?"

Eyes showing warm interest and love, and a bright smile.

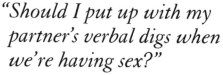

"Is it good to talk when we're having sex?"

Some couples like to, but if your partner prefers quiet do as she prefers.

"Should I put up with my partner's verbal digs when we're having sex?"

No, nor at any time. If they are angry or frustrated, talk about it and resolve the problem, but lovemaking's not the time.

"I'm conscious of my posh accent. Can I still sound sexy?"

Any accent can be sexy as long as your voice is warm and loving and you keep it low and not strident.

"Is it ok to whisper sweet nothings?"

Yes, they're great, and they mean a lot.

"Should I get used to talking dirty just because my partner likes it?"

Unless you're uncomfortable with it, yes do. It will add to his pleasure and probably yours too.

"Is it ok to answer the phone when we're making love?"

Unless you're expecting your children to phone, no. In fact, turn phones off before you start. Your partner needs your full attention.

"What are the two sexiest things to say?"

Mmmmm… and *You're amazing.*

"Which is the best place in the house for lovemaking?"

Usually somewhere very comfortable and warm, such as your bed or on the sofa or a soft rug on the living room floor. Occasionally less likely places, like the stairs, can be exciting.

"Is it loving to play music you love but your partner hates?"

No. Lovemaking is about things you both love, and that includes music.

"Why is music so sexy?"

Because it's all about melody and rhythm, changing tempos, crescendos and climaxes. And passion. And love.

"What's the sexiest form of exercise we can do together, apart from making love?"

Most exercise can be sexy, but dance excels because the music and movement combine in a feeling of oneness and passion.

Life stages

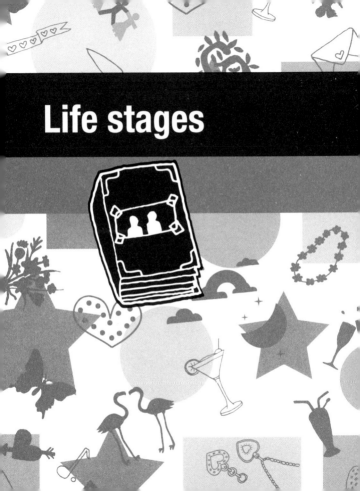

"Is it realistic to think that we'll love each other all through our lives, no matter what happens?"

Yes, if you choose to share the path of life, loving and supporting each other all along the way.

"*For me, love is everything. Does it matter that my partner has more important priorities?*"

Not if you love each other and are happy together. Love varies in importance throughout life's phases, but it can still thrive.

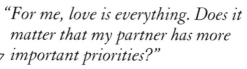

"*Will love mean I lose my freedom?*"

Only if you give it away. Love values each other's freedom and has to be freely given and freely received.

"I love my partner, but how can I know if I always will?"

If you choose to love and respect each other and do your best to keep to your promises, there's every reason to think you will keep them.

"Are there any rules of love that stay unchanging at any age?"

Yes, a mutual code of conduct that includes kindness, respect, support and a loving physical connection.

"What's your best advice for keeping love alive through all life's stages?"

Be each other's best friend.

"Will sex always be an important element of our love?"

Not necessarily, but even if at some stage you no longer have sex, the shared memory of good sex and continuing physical affection can endure and enrich your relationship for ever.

"Can you prepare yourself for relationships, and is it a good idea to do so?"

Yes and yes. Finding out what makes a good relationship tick paves the way for one and saves all manner of mistakes and regrets.

"Is being happily
married a skill?"

*Yes, and like any skill you can learn and improve
with good practice.*

"Is a good relationship
worth the effort?"

Yes, a million times worth it.

"Why should we persevere when it could be easier to live alone?"

*Because living with your loved one is a taste
of heaven on earth.*

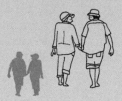

"As well as love, is there a purpose and benefit to spending our lives together?"

Yes: to share each other's experiences. Along the way you'll double the happiness and joys and halve the sorrows.

"As a couple, how can we best approach life's various stages?"

Be prepared for changes, enthusiastic about enjoying your life together and love each other the way you are at every age.

"I want my boyfriend to be the man of my whole life. Is it possible?"

Yes, but you've much growing and changing to do as you mature into adults. Enjoy your friendship and romance in the moment.

"How can life be worth living now that my girlfriend's told me it's over?"

The first time you're dumped you think you'll never get over it, but you will, surprisingly quickly, if you remember the sweetness of love, forget the pain and let yourself heal.

"How many hurts will I have or cause before I meet a life-long partner?"

You may fall in love many times before finding love that deepens, ripens and stays true. But temporary romance is lovely too, so enjoy each one.

"Should we tell our romantic, head-in-the-clouds daughter that lasting love takes a lot of hard work?"

It would be better and truer to tell her that it's about enthusiasm, effort, positivity and emotional intelligence, all of which, in the right spirit, can be pleasurable!

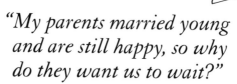

"My parents married young and are still happy, so why do they want us to wait?"

They realize now how very young they were and want you to wait for a while before making the huge commitment that fortunately worked out for them. It's your decision, but why rush it?

"How can we keep our individuality when we're so in love and together?"

Allow yourself and each other to expand individually, as that's a part of love.

"We're all over each other, which is great, but what if we swamp each other?"

You both need to breathe and so does love. Look after your individual lives as well as your romance.

"I'm trying to live up to the image he has of me, but is it right that I feel inhibited?"

No. It's fine to try to be your best self but don't inhibit the real you.

"How can I stop my boyfriend trying to make me be just like his mum?"

Tell him you're not the same as his mother and that you want to be sure he loves you the way you are.

"My partner spends more time with his best friend than with me. Is my resentment unreasonable?"

No. Your individual friendships are valuable, but your relationship with each other is of prime importance. Compromise to find a balance that you're both happy with.

"My parents dislike each other and are always rowing. With this background can I ever have a loving relationship?"

Yes. You can choose not to be like your parents and instead to get on well with people, especially your partner.

"Can friends help love along?"

Yes. Friends who are glad for your happiness together and who believe in lasting love will encourage your love to thrive.

"Should we socialize together?"

Yes, as often as you can. It's great for a couple to share the happiness of being with people that they are comfortable with.

"How can I deal with friends who expect me to chat on the phone all evening even though I'm in a relationship?"

Switch on the answer-phone or say, *I can't chat now*, except for one or two evenings a week when you can catch up with their calls.

"I hate it when he constantly texts friends when we're together. Am I unreasonable?"

No, you are not. To keep on doing this is rude, and if you want to look after your love and relationship you need to pay attention to each other.

"How can I deal with my jealousy of my partner's love for her friends?"

Dissolve your jealousy by recognizing and respecting her right to have friends.

"I don't mind my partner having friends, but should I try to make sure I'm number one?"

No. It's better to stop comparing friendship love with your love for each other altogether. They are different.

★ "How can I help my best friend feel less left out now I have a boyfriend?"

It will help her accept that relationships take time and to adjust quickly if you remember to speak with her or see her regularly.

"How should I react to my friends teasing me because I'm so in love?"

If it's warm, loving teasing, enjoy it. If it's not, ignore it.

"We both have friends, and although he gets on with mine, I don't know what he sees in his. Couldn't he give them up and share mine?"

Be glad he enjoys and values his own friendships and resist the urge to criticize them.

"My friends' partners are wealthier than mine. Will feelings of inferiority sabotage our love?"

Only if you let them. Wealth won't make either of you a better person, and love is about character, not money.

"Now I'm married, there aren't enough hours in the day to do all the things I like such as going to the gym and spending time with family, friends and my partner. How can I fit everything in?"

Make time with your partner your chief priority, followed by your other loved ones. Organize time to yourself, too, and manage it carefully to include your chosen pastimes.

"As long as I don't hurt my partner, is it all right to have an affair?"

No. You would be breaking your promise of fidelity and would almost certainly hurt her.

"Surely an affair can strengthen a marriage?"

Extremely rarely. It is far better to find out what is missing in your marriage and to resolve this.

"My wife doesn't think her affair was wrong, although she's sorry it hurt me. Is adultery morally wrong?"

Yes. In our culture, at least, it's generally considered wrong.

"Can you love two people equally?"

Yes, but not in exactly the same way. All people are different, so your feelings towards them can never be identical.

"I'm having an affair and it's tearing me apart. How can we be together but be sure to avoid hurting our partners?"

You can't.

"I love two men. Must I choose between them?"

Yes, unless all three of you are happy with a ménage à trois.

"He adores his mother. How can I ever match up?"

There is no need. He loves you both but in very different ways. Be glad that he loves his mother.

"Her mother is very critical of me: for instance, she challenges almost everything I say. Should I just avoid her?"

Get to know and like her, and let her know that you aren't stealing her daughter's love from her. In time she'll relax and warm to you.

"For my partner's sake, how can I resist my family's huge demands on my time?"

Firmly, lovingly and gently make it clear that now you have a partner your time with them is no longer unlimited.

"My partner is constantly dragged into family rows and expects me to be involved too. Should I?"

No. Theses are not your conflicts, so listen sympathetically but keep out of them.

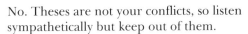

"Will my husband still love me as I begin to get larger?"

He'll cherish you even more now that you're you plus a little one, who's a bit of both of you!

"Will I feel the same about my partner now that I'm going to be a mum?"

In addition to loving him as your lover and partner, you will love him as the father of your baby, so your love will grow and be even more joyful.

"I love my partner, but, now I'm pregnant, how can I lose a worrying feeling that I'm obligated to stay with him?"

Accept willingly the feeling of duty to your baby and partner, and it will become joyful.

"Can my partner possibly feel the same love for me and our baby as I feel for them?"

Paternal and maternal love have their own nuances, but you share the same tenderness and delight in each other and in your baby.

"How can we find time for each other when being a mum takes so much time and energy?"

Set aside small periods when you're one-to-one, and make these times a daily pleasure to reassure you both how important you are to each other.

"She used to look after me, but now we've a baby I have to look after her. Am I incredibly selfish and the only man to find this hard?"

No and no! Throughout life you'll take turns at being supportive. Try to enjoy both roles.

"Do all new parents feel scared?"

Most do. Soothe your fears with cheerful anticipation of the love and joy that lie ahead.

"I remember how good together my parents seemed when I was a kid. Can we seem like that to our children?"

Yes, by showing your love for each other and being united as parents too.

"Can we keep the magic of being lovers now that we're parents?"

Yes. Remember what a treasure love is and how precious you are to each other.

"We're daunted by the responsibility of being parents. Will our feelings spoil our love?"

Not as long as you stand together, united. Then your new responsibilities will add a wonderful new dimension to your love.

"How can I make love when I'm so exhausted?"

Remember that lovemaking is a relaxing pleasure, and grab the opportunity when your baby has a nap rather than when you're sleepy at bedtime.

"We waste whole evenings moaning about work. Is it good to get it off our chests?"

Not all evening! Offloading worries can be helpful, but limit your complaints to a few minutes so they don't spoil your time together.

"How can we stop our dislike of certain colleagues from clouding our leisure time too?"

When you're at home forget about them. When you're at work be charming to them.

"Am I selfish to insist on some me-time, even though he's busy too?"

It's sensible, not selfish, to stand up for something you need. If you don't do this your resentment could accumulate.

"How can I stop my wife from humiliating me because I've disappointed her financially and professionally?"

Ask her to appreciate you as the person you are instead of a money-making machine.

"Now that we don't want any more children and our careers take all our energy, is it ok to forget about sex?"

And miss out on all that potential giving and receiving of pleasure, intimacy, ecstasy and, last but not least, relaxation?

"We rush in and out, grazing on the run. Would eating together be good for our ailing relationship?"

Yes, it would be great because sharing one of life's pleasures will draw you closer together. Take your time to relish the food and each other's company.

"When I lost my job my partner said he'd support me, but he's becoming reluctant to give me money. Surely he should be happy to keep me?"

It's hard to keep two people financially afloat. Love is working together as a team.

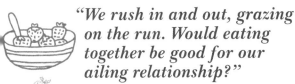

"I thought my fiancé would be successful, but he's given up his career for a less demanding job he loves. Should I still marry him, even though he has no prospects?"

Money won't make you happy. Discover the value of his personality and the love you share before making a decision.

"How can I help my partner be happy at work?"

Be his mentor by listening, taking an interest, helping him think clearly and encouraging him along the path he takes.

"My partner doesn't want me to work, even though he knows my career is important to me. Should I give it up to please him?"

No. Love is helping each other find all-round satisfaction.

"How can I soothe my partner's fear that my new promotion will sap all my energy?"

Agree to be pleasant and supportive to each other, even when you're tired, and make an effort not to take your work problems home with you.

"We're both in competitive jobs. Is it ok to be competitive with each other?"

No, because it could be divisive. If you see yourselves as a team and encourage each other's success your relationship will be a winner.

"My profession is what I am, so how can I not put it before my marriage?"

By realizing that while it's important to you, it isn't you. Recognize and love your real self and your intrinsic, vital part in your loving relationship.

"Which should be our chief priority, our relationship or our careers?"

Your careers earn your living and give you a sense of achievement, but your love and relationship are hugely important too, so care for both.

"The long hours I work are strangling our relationship, but what can I do?"

Work the hours you're supposed to work. Your employers will accept it if you work well and enthusiastically, and your relationship will benefit hugely.

"Will balancing work and our home life ever be easier?"

It's always challenging as you adjust to changes, but less so the more you appreciate the benefits of a happier relationship.

"As a home worker I have less time with my partner because when friends call in I have to work on into the evening. What can I do?"

Put a flag or sign on your door saying, Working: please don't disturb!

"My partner hides it when he's scared of anything. Should I ignore his fear too?"

No. Show him that you're supportive with a hug or by saying, Is there anything I can do?

"How can I soothe my partner's stress?"

With love in the shape of small, loving gestures and quiet understanding.

"When she's depressed, my partner says there's nothing I can do. Is there something?"

Love her. Love finds the best way to ease the path through depression.

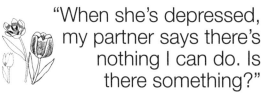

"I'm having pre-marriage doubts. How can I promise to love her in sickness when I don't know if I could really cope?"

Love will cope. And caring for her will make you feel good.

"We feel at a loose end now the children have left home. How can we lose this empty-nest feeling?"

By grabbing the chance to do things together and enjoy each other's company, just as you did before you started your family.

"When we were young my partner made me so happy. Why doesn't he bother any more?"

It was too much of a responsibility. Create your own happiness and self-fulfilment and love him for being his own self.

"How can I help my partner through a mid-life confidence crisis?"

Every day, at least, think of and tell her something you genuinely love or admire about her.

"Should I tell my husband that I've changed now I'm older, for instance, I have very different views about world politics today, or should I pretend to be the same?"

Be true to yourself and to each other so that your love can be true and strong.

"Now the children have grown up our principal role as parents is virtually obsolete. How can we stop a feeling of pointlessness from invading our marriage?"

Instead of yearning for roles past, concentrate on your roles now. As a couple you are lovers and best friends; independently, you are both potentially vibrantly active, fulfilled mature people. Create the roles you want and give them your best, and life will regain its purpose and satisfaction.

"We're bitter that we haven't done as well as our friends. How can we stop this resentment coming between us?"

Adore each other, fill your lives with kindness and appreciate your blessings. These are the keys to happiness, whatever our material success.

"Now we're financially secure life has lost its challenge and our marriage feels flat too. How can we bring back our zest?"

Set yourselves new challenges in a shared interest or sport.

"We want to revitalize our life together. How can we spur ourselves to make the changes we'd like?"

Together make lists of your goals and short- and mid-term steps towards them. Take the first step and you'll be away.

"Suddenly we're seeing each other as whole people rather than Mum and Dad. Is it usual to feel shy?"

Yes, it often happens. Remember the excitement of getting to know each other when you first met and enjoy it all over again now.

"Life has become a boring mixture of domesticity and work. Where did our passion for life go?"

It's still there. Give it some air to breathe again by cultivating boundless curiosity: about life, our world and what makes you both tick. Irrepressible fascination is irresistibly beguiling!

"We know we're lucky to enjoy our relationship and life together, but how can we lose a feeling of guilt?"

Do some voluntary work together. As well as helping other people, it will be satisfying and will strengthen your bond.

"Does everyone feel trapped when they've been married for years?"

Not if they remember that they chose to be together in the first place and make that choice again, every day.

"I've gone off sex. Do I have to see it as a duty just to keep my husband with me?"

See lovemaking not as an irksome duty but as the beautiful promise you made to each other: With my body I cherish you.

> *"Do I support my partner's wish to take early retirement even though it will mean less money?"*

Help him clarify all the implications, including the financial ones. Tell him you'll back him to the hilt, whatever he decides is best.

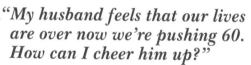

> *"My husband feels that our lives are over now we're pushing 60. How can I cheer him up?"*

Point out that you've potentially the best third of your lives to come. And have fun together maximizing your opportunities.

"Now we're older, would we both be happier in other relationships?"

There is no guarantee that you will be, so rather than falling for the idea that the grass is greener elsewhere, why not look after your own garden and, together, make it beautiful.

"How can I get my husband to accept I'm menopausal and too hot to *spoon* like we used to?"

Reassure him that it's a temporary side-effect of the menopause and that you still love him very much. Get close again as soon as the hot flushes cease, and meanwhile, whenever you're cool, snuggle up to him.

"Will my wife be moody during the menopause, and how can I help?"

Some women find the hormonal adjustments cause emotional ups and downs. Your understanding and love will be a huge support to her.

"At the age of 45 my husband's yearning for adventure. Is it mid-life crisis?"

It could be. Help him recognize his feelings and widen his general horizons while continuing to appreciate and nurture the love and bond you share.

"My partner's discovered a natural talent for the art I've always struggled to learn. Should I give up?"

Goodness no. Enjoy your work and be glad that he's found a new talent. Step back gracefully while you bask in his reflected glory.

"How can I get used to my husband being at home when he retires?"

Accept that there will be some changes to your routine, enjoy his company and encourage each other's continuing independence.

"How can we avoid becoming crotchety and old?"

Protect your zest for life: every moment, every day. If you love each other, your friends and your world, you'll age youthfully and beautifully!

"Could the many sorrows we've experienced throughout our lives have enriched our wellbeing and love?"

Yes. Sorrow often brings wisdom, compassion and a deeper appreciation of love and each other.

"The mortgage is paid off and the children are all working. Do we still need each other?"

More than ever before, for now you have the opportunity to be of prime importance to each other. Cherish it and cherish each other.

"Are we daft to still hold hands now we're old?"

No, extremely sane! Holding hands affirms your love, feels nice and is a great example to all of us of lasting love.

"When I look at my wrinkles in the mirror I'm puzzled: how can my husband love me when I've changed so much?"

When you love someone, the signs of age don't matter and can increase tenderness.

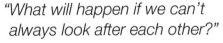

"What will happen if we can't always look after each other?"

To put your minds at rest, talk about the future care you may need with your children, others who are close to you and, if you can and you think it necessary, any local government social services department.

"Can we always feel sexy, even if we live to 100?"

Yes, you may do, and even if you do not you can still recall the wonder to mind and bask in the warmth and joy any time you want.

"As we get on very well with them, should we ask my wife's elderly parents to live with us?"

If everyone likes the idea it could work well for you all. Talk it through in as much detail as you can and take expert advice about the logistics.

"We anticipate having lots more time for each other when we retire. But what if one of us dies?"

Plans and dreams are lovely, but most important of all is to love and make time for each other now.

"How can I bear it if my partner dies before me?"

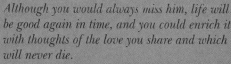

Although you would always miss him, life will be good again in time, and you could enrich it with thoughts of the love you share and which will never die.

Fading love

"Are we wasting our time trying to understand why our feelings have changed and what, if anything, we can do about it?"

No, it's great to recognize what's happened, but not all at once. Address aspects one by one and don't overanalyze. Sort it out with love.

"How can we still fancy each other when we know each other's most unappealing characteristics?"

Don't slob about. Out of respect and love for each other, behave sensitively and be attractive.

"Although we are considering splitting up we still make love. Does this mean we still love each other?"

Sexually, yes. Enough for a full relationship, no. Save your relationship by putting your all into getting on well and loving other aspects of each other besides sex.

"When I'd gone off him, he wanted me, and now he's losing interest in me, I realize I love him. Why are we so perverse?"

Because you value love only when it's a challenge. Reset your values, be loving and appreciate each other's love.

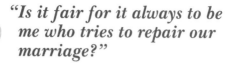

"Is it fair for it always to be me who tries to repair our marriage?"

No. You should aim for a 50–50 balance with lots of give and take on both sides.

"She says she wants to separate for a while to give herself space. Is she ending our relationship?"

It's more likely she's confused about her path of life and about your relationship and hopes to clarify how she thinks on her own.

"Why does he think I don't love him because I want to do my own thing in my precious leisure time?"

He feels as if he's way down your priorities. Be companionable much more often. Your love is worth it.

"I don't want to break up, but how can I get back the loving feeling I used to have?"

To feel loving again, be loving.

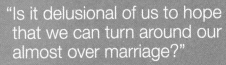

"Is it delusional of us to hope that we can turn around our almost over marriage?"

No. It's very possible, for there is no last-minute rescue that mutual love and determination cannot accomplish.

"How can we reverse the downward slide of our relationship?"

Switch from apathy, unkindness or neglect to full-on mutual care, kindness and interest.

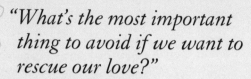

"What's the most important thing to avoid if we want to rescue our love?"

Criticism scars souls and has
no place in a loving relationship.

"Can we regain the vibrancy of our early love?"

Yes. Whenever your marriage loses its piquancy, season it with interest, attention and full-on love.

"He wanted a trial separation and has moved out. I desperately want him back. Should I keep contacting him?"

It's fine to contact him occasionally, but he's
more likely to come back to you if he
doesn't feel pressured.

"When he left me he told me to give him space to think. But how will he know I still love him and want him back if I don't say anything?"

Tell him you do love him to set your mind at rest. Then quietly stand back and respect the space he's chosen.

"What do we need to do to mend our marriage?"

Give it a transfusion of intention, attention and, of course, love.

"We've sorted out the problems between us and want to rebuild our love and friendship. Will it take years to regain our original rapport?"

You can repair it seamlessly in a gradual or swift process. Love flows of its own accord when you enable it.

"We'd like to separate, but how do we part when we share lovely possessions and friends?"

You are free to stay put and love each other as well as your lifestyle, or to part and dismantle it all.

"He complains about my nagging, but what else can I do when he doesn't do his fair share?"

If your first mention is ignored, ask again. If he still hesitates, talk about why and solve it as a team without batting complaints at each other.

"We've fallen out of love. Should we accept it or try to revive our romance?"

If you had a good thing going between you and would like to have it back, it's worth restoring. If not, let it go.

"Is there any reason not to be nice to each other, even though we're separating?"

None. Relating to each other well is a choice you can always make.

"I don't matter to my husband or our children. Has their love for me completely died?"

Sit them down (insist they make time) and tell them that you feel you don't matter to them. Seeing the impact on you of their neglect will be a wake-up call for their love.

"He thinks I don't care about him any more. How can I convince him I do?"

Tell him you love him with all your heart. Show him. Be there for him. Most of all, value him so much he can't help but know it.

"Is there a formula for a happy, lasting marriage?"

There's no set formula because every relationship is unique, but there are many qualities that help love thrive, such as interest in each other, understanding and loyalty

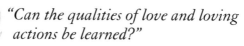

"Can the qualities of love and loving actions be learned?"

Yes. They are learnable skills, which need to be repeated to continue to thrive.

"Aren't good relationships naturally formed?"

Often yes, but all happy couples are extremely caring of their relationship.

"How can we feel so negative towards each other when once we adored each other?"

When love disappears, negativity fills the gap. Replace it with positivity by remembering why you loved each other.

"Why do people fall out of love?"

Because they find they're not right for each other or don't look after their love.

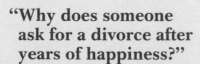

"Why does someone ask for a divorce after years of happiness?"

Their emotions, reactions, needs or aspirations may have changed, and these changes need to be lovingly noticed and adjusted to.

"Is it normal to feel disappointed?"

High expectations can be tyrants. Love is about adjusting together so that your marriage evolves a form and pattern that works for you both.

"Although we'd otherwise separate, we've agreed to stay together because of the children. Could we ever enjoy our marriage again for its own sake?"

Yes. When responsibility holds a couple together it often, to their surprise, develops into love and enjoyable companionship again.

"Why does she see any closeness, a quick kiss, hug or even a one-to-one conversation, like an opportunity for sex?"

She doesn't understand that closeness and intimacy can, and should often, be non-sexual.

"How can I stop him making unwelcome sexual demands whenever we're close?"

Explain that it's uplifting and healing to be intimate with no sexual expectation and that it is as vital to your relationship as your sexual connection.

"Why does he always tell me what to do?"

He's confusing love with domination. Hug him and tell him he doesn't need to dominate you; that you want to love him for his own self on an equal and fair basis.

"Instead of loving each other, why do we find ourselves on a slippery slope of sarcasm and other cutting comments that are destroying our love?"

Love isn't about harming and destroying, it's about healing and creating and maintaining rapport. Try being nice to each other and supportive and encouraging. It will make a huge difference to your life together and build love instead of destroying it.

"How can we stop demolishing each other's confidence by ridiculing every comment or opinion?"

When you're on the brink of lashing out, pause to think and only then state your point of view calmly and reasonably.

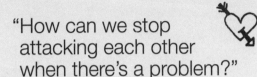

"How can we stop attacking each other when there's a problem?"

You must remember to focus on the problem instead of each other.

"Could my caustic sarcasm and wit erode my partner's love?"

Yes, if it's directed at him personally. Be witty by all means, but in a general context so your partner can laugh with you without feeling put down.

"We mostly do our own thing socially. Would it be good for our relationship to go out together?"

Yes, just the two of you. It's intimate and good to share life outside your home.

"We're both too old to change. Should we accept it's over and move on?"

It's never too late to change; you both could. You hold happiness in your own hands right now.

"How can we avoid well-meant discussions turning into mud-slinging fights?"

Listen carefully to each other's point of view and take time to think about them in a fair, positive light.

"Our sex life petered out for no particular reason. What would it take to regenerate it?"

The shared wish to, a gentle sense of humour, mutual everyday caring and plenty of romance and tenderness.

"When he has a glowering face, how can I avoid sinking into depression too?"

Agree that you'll both smile more and be nice to each other. Positivity soon comes naturally, and it's astonishingly therapeutic.

"There's no problem as such, so why does our marriage seem slightly grey?"

You are the creators of your relationship. Choose a palette of bright shades to paint a picture of love and happiness.

"Why don't we do things for each other any more?"

After the first flush of love, loving acts take thought, so decide and remember to behave lovingly. It always feels fantastic, no matter how long you've been together.

"After years of neglect, how can we care for each other again?"

Just as neglect digs a chasm between you, so attention and gestures of care close it up again and enable love.

"We don't notice each other any more, so what's the point of being together?"

Love, pure and simple. Look after your relationship and appreciate it so it's a seam of gold underpinning your lives.

"Why do we disagree more and more frequently when we used to get on so well?"

It's a habit. Break it by stopping fighting and instead focus on love and the other positive aspects of your life together.

"We thought our love was strong enough to last. Why did our feelings change?"

Feelings usually do fluctuate over the years, and if love is to survive the changes, you need to stick by it with determined perseverance.

"Our love isn't as intense as it used to be. What can we do to hold our relationship together?"

Fight apathy with all your hearts and pledge to keep your love strong and true.

"How can I accept my partner's annoying traits?"

Try seeing them in a different way, as you did when you were first in love. For instance, instead of calling him lazy, love how laid back he is.

"We used to make each other laugh until the tears rolled down our faces. Where did our ability to laugh go?"

Complacency set in. Start amusing each other again, for humour is love's heartbeat and an aphrodisiac.

"We're busy, busy, busy and have no time for each other. How do we get off the treadmill?"

You step off it confidently and give yourselves permission to be idle.

"Why do we, quite unintentionally, dampen each other's spirits?"

You've fallen into a negative pattern. Instead, brighten each other up with loving gestures and by having fun and doing things together.

"On the rare nights we both stay in, why do we feel like strangers?"

Because you're so rarely on your own together and because you're not making an effort to enjoy the intimacy. So spend more time together and consciously enjoy each other's company and closeness.

"I'm so dissatisfied with our marriage. Should we opt out?"

No. Dissatisfaction is reversible. Describe your respective visions of an ideal day in a loving relationship, and then set about making each other's dream reality. The chances are it won't take much.

"Why can't my partner accept that I'm a naturally impatient person?"

Because it's so hard to live with this habit. Cultivate patience and learn to release and deal with your anger and impatience safely.

"My partner thinks it's soppy to show affection, but I miss it. Is he right?"

He's misinformed and missing out. Affection is love in action.

"Although he's forgiven me for something mean I did, he says he'll never understand it. I've tried to explain. What more can I do?"

Point out that compassion is as important as forgiveness and ask him to stop judging you.

"My partner's as likely to let me down as not. How can I make her be more dependable?"

You can't force her. But if she realizes that dependability is pretty much essential to a good relationship she might try to be reliable. If not, a lapse of reliability on your part might wake her up.

"When did we stop talking to each other?"

Probably it began a long while ago and happened so gradually that you didn't notice. Now reverse the trend.

"We've forgiven each other for the affairs we had. How can we stop the continuing suspicion?"

By letting it go and believing in each other. You have nothing to lose and peace of mind to gain.

"We've both become touchy. Are we sliding towards separation?"

Regard over-sensitivity as an antibody to love. Heal what's wrong between you to rebuild your relationship's health.

"We never go out nowadays. Why have we got so boring?"

Is laziness the reason? At least once a week check out what's going on locally or afar, choose and book. Dating is an ongoing compliment to each other, inspiring and uniting you.

"When we're at home in the evenings we love to watch television. Is that boring?"

No, it's one of life's simplest pleasures, especially if you snuggle up together.

"Is television the scourge of modern relationships?"

If you choose to watch things that engage you both and get you talking it's a surprisingly uniting pastime to share.

"His arrogance annoys me so. Why does he always have to be right?"

Speaking without bitterness, point out his habit each time it recurs. Recognizing what he does will help him give it up.

"Why doesn't she see it emasculates me when she makes all the decisions?"

Tell her she's bright and sassy but that you are too and that you're going to take turns at taking the lead.

"Why have we become like strangers lodging in the same house?"

You've neglected the art of companionship. Start taking an interest and pleasure in each other's company. That's love.

"How can we stop my tendency to be a control freak coming between us?"

Abandon it for the most part. You'll find that it's a huge relief to give up sole responsibility for everything.

"The way we speak to each other is killing our love. Is it normal to speak roughly and rudely?"

No. You need to talk about how it's become the norm in your relationship and agree to be kind, supportive and loving to each other. When you get the hang of it, it will transform your relationship.

"He needs everyone else to love him, but ignores me. How can I get his attention and love?"

Alert him to the fact that the love you share is dying of neglect. Put your all, both of you, into bringing it back to life.

"How can we stop feeling constantly disappointed that our marriage isn't perfect?"

By remembering that flaws and ups and downs are all part of a growing, complex work in progress. Enjoy the whole picture.

"How can I stop her behaving as if she owns me?"

Tell her you're her partner, not her pet.

"When problems arise how can we change our instant reaction of blaming each other?"

By thinking through together how the problem can best be tackled.

"We've tried to change each other and ourselves. Could it be that we can't do either?"

Yes, so don't try to be people you're not. Be your true selves in the best, most loving way you can be.

"When we feel frustrated with life generally it rubs off on our relationship. Can we avoid this?"

Yes, by realizing that frustrations are part of life, including relationships, and that it's ok that your relationship is affected by your life.

"As we can't undo what's been said and done, is it most sensible to give up on our marriage?"

Not if you can forgive and, in future, rise to the challenge of resolving recurring or new issues. And remember to love each other, full on.

"How can I stop my partner deriding characteristics about me that he once loved?"

Point out how harmful this habit is, and ask him to love you the way you are.

"We don't want to break up, but how can we happily stay together?"

By recognizing the tremendous potential and goodness of your love for each other, then putting it into practice on a daily basis.

"**Whatever I do, she puts her oar in and changes it. For example, last night I'd booked a table at a restaurant for us and some friends, and she changed our booking to somewhere else. Should I tolerate her meddling?**"

No. Point out to her that such interference is a devious form of control and ask her to notice and check the tendency. In general, aim to liaise as much as possible on decisions.

"Could therapy help save our relationship?"

Yes, if you both want to save it.

"*How can therapy improve things between us?*"

You'll both learn a lot from it and can put what you learn into practice so that you can adjust and perhaps transform your relationship.

"Talking about our relationship is confusing. Would therapy help us find a way forward?"

Yes. It will help you clarify issues and identify potential solutions.

"We get so emotional and angry about our problems. What good can a therapist do?"

A counsellor will mediate between you and enable you to talk positively, constructively and, above all, lovingly again.

"Does the model or style of therapy matter?"

No. Research shows that all methods can be effective, so the main thing is to feel comfortable with it.

"Why does she always think I'm angry at her when it's something else entirely?"

It's her natural or learned response. Therapy could help her understand and cope rationally and constructively with her own and others' anger.

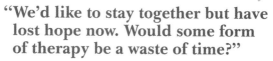

"We'd like to stay together but have lost hope now. Would some form of therapy be a waste of time?"

No, because it will give you hope.

"We're getting divorced, but it will take some time to sell our house. Can we both live there until we do?"

If the divorce is a mutual decision and neither of you is hurt, there is no reason not to share the house until it's sold. Otherwise, the less painful way would be for one of you to move out, but do take legal advice first.

"My partner says he doesn't know what love is. Although I've tried, I can't help him. Should I agree to his wish to separate?"

Yes. A loving relationship takes two.

"I broke up with my partner, then realized that I still love him. Why won't he make it up?"

He's confused and unwilling to put himself in a position where he might be hurt again.

"How can I prove I want to make our relationship work again when she won't even answer my calls?"

Write to her saying you're sorry you broke up and would like to get back together. If she doesn't respond, accept that it's over.

"Is divorce always a failure?"

Not if, despite your best efforts, you're simply incompatible. But if one or both of you are nasty and inconsiderate then, yes, it is, and sadly an avoidable one.

"How did I make such a mess of what started out so well?"

A relationship takes two to make, two to break.

"Can anything make up for the love I've lost?"

Yes. Be glad for the love you shared that gave you so much pleasure and enriched your life and personality.

"How can we move on from the sense of failure and guilt?"

Logically and positively reflect that divorce isn't a failure when it's the best way forward.

"How will I ever get over losing her?"

If you allow yourself to heal you will find that the pain eases and eventually disappears completely.

"Was all the love we had together a waste of time?"

Love is never a waste. If you refuse to be bitter but instead are glad for the love and joy you shared, more will flow into your life.

"I bumped into my ex recently and our old attraction flared up. Living together didn't work, but would it be ok to enjoy sex again?"

Only if neither of you have promised to be faithful to present partners and you're sure that your fling won't renew the hurt of the original break-up.

"I worry that my partner might have sex with his ex-wife when he drops their children off at her place. Can I believe his promise he won't?"

Yes, that's what trust is and, unlike distrust, it's a pleasant emotion.

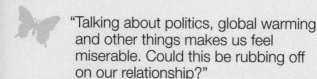

"Talking about politics, global warming and other things makes us feel miserable. Could this be rubbing off on our relationship?"

Yes. Glum talk makes us glum, so cut out the grim chat and think, talk and love positively and constructively instead.

"I still love my ex-partner and desperately want a reconciliation. Is it possible and would it work?"

Yes, if he wants it to as well and you're both prepared to resolve what went wrong and rebuild your love and rapport on an ongoing daily basis.

"Is it possible to grow back together?"

Yes. With loving commitment and a little energy you can connect and bond again.

"Our friends don't think there's much chance of our marriage working second time around. Could we win despite the odds against it?"

If you both put your all into your love it's a certainty.

Accents, voice 337

acceptance 151, 165, 279, 409, 419

activities 26

adultery *see* affairs

adventure 382

advice 206, 215, 216, 251

affairs 164, 280, 295, 301, 356–7, 413

affection, showing 64, 328, 344, 412

affirmations 54

affordable pleasures 180

ageing 79, 245, 277, 381, 386

agencies 100

aggression 13, 208

agreeing to differ 252

alertness 283

allowances, making 229

alone, time *see* time apart

always, use of word 213

ambitiousness 55

anger
  acknowledging 163
  arguments 259, 260
  dealing with 106, 143, 153, 164
  therapy 421, 422

anxiety 15, 62, 69, 247

apart, promoting love when 262

apathy 393, 408

apologizing 175, 250, 252, 260

appreciation
  blessings 376
  complacency 229, 248
  relationships 407
  self-esteem 75
  whole person 77, 366

arguments
  anger 259, 260
  avoiding 405
  closeness 250
  damage 142
  dealing with 159, 165
  exhausting 163
  health 21
  helped by 45
  listening 234
  opinions 140
  past fights 162
  replaying 256, 259
  shouting 186
  silence 174
  sleeping separately 260
  solutions 141

tiredness 178
arousal 20, 29, 311, 323
arrogance 253, 415
art 383
aspects of love 10, 177
assertiveness 152
assumptions about love 190
attention 74, 187, 209, 407
attraction 17, 92–5
attractive people 83
attractive qualities 108

Bad habits 141
bad moods 189
bad temper 153
being there, trust 268
best friends, being each
    other's 343
betrayal 274, 303
big-headedness 68
bitterness 137
blaming 216, 418
blind dates 110
blind trust 282
body, self-image 30, 66, 83
body clocks 208
body language 196, 204, 212,
    262

books 176
boredom
    laziness 414
    mid-life 378
    with partner 131, 179, 230
    sex 324, 325
bossiness 200, 215, 216, 402
bragging 107
brains, sex 316
brainteasers 25
breakfasts 239, 240
breaking objects 230
breaking up 422–3
bullying 13, 153, 166
business, away on 193
busy lives 235, 410
buttons, pushing each other's
    174

Careers 68, 75, 100, 369
    see also work
casual sex 306
celebrations 157
celibacy 28
change
    dealing with 62
    feelings 390, 408
    life stages 346

potential for 163, 405
relationships 74
trust 296, 297
checking identity 102
chemicals 17
children 132
chores 34–5
see also tasks
church weddings 38
clarity 198
climaxes *see* orgasms
closeness 401
code of conduct, love as 343
commitment 40, 126–8, 284, 288
communication 184–221
companionship 416
compassion 51, 232, 412
compatibility 41
competitiveness 67, 68, 369
complacency 229, 409
complaints 211, 365
complexity, relationships 249
compliments 89, 195
compromise 258
confidence
boosting 64, 77, 174
decisions 48
demolishing 403

honesty 52
lacking 56
sex 88
see also self-confidence
connection 177, 184, 205, 275
constructive comments 251
contact 118, 203, 394
contempt 211
contentment 44, 71, 226
contrasts, love 224
controlling behaviour 79, 416
cooking 171, 265
courage 270
creating love 238, 252
creativity 197
criticism 57, 194, 211, 213, 394
crosswords 25
crying 159

Dancing 23, 151, 339
dating 105–11, 414
see also meeting people
dating sites 101
death 387
decisions 48, 415, 420
deepening of love 15
defensiveness 159, 189

demands 207
dementia 169
demonstrative behaviour 43, 185
dependability 275, 293, 413
desire, sex 18–19, 27, 318–20
detachment 204
differences 45, 160, 165, 173, 252
difficult times 150
disagreements 208, 407
disappointment 173, 400, 417
discussions 405
disparaging talk 113
disputes *see* arguments
dissatisfaction 411
distrust 269, 284, 298, 300, 303
divorce 400, 422, 424
DIY 33
domination 402
doormats, treatment as 112
doubts 70, 302
down, feeling 191
dreams 203
dress 31, 110
dullness 49

Early love 238, 394
eating *see* mealtimes
eccentricities 22, 152
eloquence 188
e-mail 102, 103
emotions *see* feelings
empty-nest feeling 374
encouragement 187
end of relationships 347
endearments 196
endorphins 18, 20
engagement rings 130
engagements 126
e-pals 111
erogenous zones 333
erotic dress 31
erotic oasis 32
etiquette 109
exaggeration 101
exercise 65, 339
ex-partners 105, 426
expectations 117, 400
explanations 175
exploring relationships 229
expressing love 97, 265
eye contact 262, 335, 336

Facial expressions 336
fading love 390–427
failure 424, 425
faith 155
faithfulness
  affairs 356
  commitment 288
  helping 297
  promises 274, 287
  trust 271, 281, 283
fallibility 280
falling in love 114–15
falling out of love 391–5, 399
familiarity 179, 230, 232
families 351, 358–9
fancying someone 93, 390
fantasies, sexual 85
fascination, reviving 242
fault-finding in public 161
fear
  hiding 372
  jealousy 295
  of losing freedom 127, 235, 342
  of losing identity 41, 42
  relationships 61, 62, 175, 247
  of trust 271

feedback *see* criticism
feelings 52, 211, 257, 390, 393
fidelity *see* faithfulness
fights *see* arguments
finance *see* money
finding love 100–3
first dates 106, 110, 111
first sight, love at 92
flaws 113
flexibility 153
flirting 282
flowers 97, 122
forever, love lasting 95
forgiveness 167, 174, 259, 412, 413, 419
freedom, fear of losing 127, 235, 342
frequency, sex 82, 85, 86, 312–13, 326, 328
friends 61, 100, 351–5
friendship
  best friends 343
  compatibility 41
  grow into love 110, 112
  just friends 121
  maintaining 48, 72
frustrations 418
fun

cultivating 24, 157, 232
negativity 410
playfulness 236
romance 98
trust 269
furniture 148

Games 25
gifts 122
glumness 426
God 36, 38
going out 77, 404, 414
going steady 133
good atmosphere 109
'good in bed' 31
good comments 14
good relationships 344, 345, 399
gratitude 424, 425
greater goodness 37, 38
grievances 167
growing 42
growing apart 169, 233
growing back together 169, 427
guilt 425

Haemoglobin 335
hands, holding 383
happiness
creating own 374
effect on others 21, 156
increasing 60
maintaining 225, 233, 254
marriage 345
relationships 12
self-esteem 59, 67
trust 303
hard work, marriage 157
harmony 150–4
harsh words 142, 198
healing talk 201
health 20–1
helplessness 197
higher power 37
hobbies 26, 35, 100, 175
see also interests
holding hands 39, 383
holidays 240, 309
home-coming, sense of 45
home workers 371
honesty 52, 201, 211, 253, 285–9
hope, relationships 260, 422
hormones 20, 317

horrid behaviour
    see unkindness
hot flushes 381
houses, buying 128
housework 34–5
hugs 39, 192, 226
hurt feelings 197

I love you' 202, 291
ideals of love 229
identity 41, 42, 102, 349–50
illness 28, 80, 150, 319, 373
impatience 412
impulsive behaviour 231
in-love feeling 119, 318
independence 118
individuality 42, 51, 349
    see also uniqueness
infatuation 68, 116–19
infidelity see affairs
informed, keeping each other
    170
inspiring self-esteem 62–79
intercourse, difficult 314
interest in each other 242
interests 26, 100, 264
    see also hobbies
interference 420

interior decorating 148
interior design 149
intimacy 41, 179, 401, 402
introductions 100
irritations 19, 137–43, 247,
    257

Jealousy 294–5, 353
jeopardizing love 218
jobs see careers; work
joy 11, 157, 238

Keeping in touch 184, 183,
    225
kindness 16, 51, 286

Lasting love 224–65
lateness 138
later life 177
laughter 24, 98, 263, 409
laziness 414
leadership 258, 415
learning love 398
left out, feelings of being 69
leisure time 26
lies 201, 285

life, meaning of 37
life stages 342–87
lifestyle 73
liking 120
listening
  body language 188
  connection 184
  just listening 206
  not listening 167, 205
  and talking 214, 253
  time for 209
living together 32–5, 40,
  146–9, 346, 422
  see also marriage;
relationships
loneliness 121
looking at attractive people 83
loss 425
love at first sight 92
loveless relationships 252
lovemaking *see* sex
loving behaviour 172, 190,
  196, 227, 299, 406

Making up 423
manipulative behaviour 199
manners 109, 111
marriage
  avoiding 130, 131

  in church 38
  disappointment 400, 417
  fidelity 287
  floundering 160
  happiness 345, 398
  hard work 157
  improving 89
  lasting 398
  for lifetime 181
  mid-life 375
  previous 125, 292
  promises 288
  repairing 14, 76, 78, 392,
    395
  second time same partner
    427
  security 40
  share meaning of 71
  spirituality 38, 39
  timing 128
  turning it around 393
  see also living together;
relationships
martyrdom 13
massage 262, 331
maturity 44, 173, 233
me-time 365
mealtimes 147, 209, 239, 240,
  318, 367

mean words 158
meaning of life 37
meaning of love 10–17, 172
meddling 420
meeting people 100
    see also dating
memories *see* past
men, sex 310, 324
ménage à trois 357
menopause 381, 382
mental interaction 25
mid-life 374–81
mistakes 57
misunderstandings 198, 205, 210, 214
money 149, 218, 273, 367, 368, 380
monogamy 133
moods, responding to 243
mothers, of partners 358
moving in 146, 147
music 23, 330, 339
mutual sexual satisfaction 19

Nagging 141, 168, 286, 396
names 76
narcissism 51
natural self *see* real self

needs 153, 249
negativity 53, 175, 186, 209, 399, 410
neglect 393, 397, 407, 417
never, use of word 213
new acquaintances 108
new aspects of partner 73
new challenges 376
newspapers 100
nice comments 188
night sky 239
non-verbal communication 192
nurturing love 225–38

Openness 270
opinions 140, 167, 212, 242
optimists 56, 155, 161, 289
orgasms
    effect of 18, 19, 21
    faking 311
    learning 84
    thought-induced 317
    together 87
    too quickly 324
    women 323
over-dependence 50
over-sensitivity 414

own room 33

Panicky feelings 57
parenthood 362–4
parents 150, 351, 387
passion for life 378
passive aggression 138
past 124, 137, 162, 167
past lives 44
patience 292, 412
patronizing behaviour 170
perfection 117, 255, 417
perseverance 234
personal baggage 122–5
personal beliefs 155–6
personal space 127
personalities 70
pessimists 56, 155
pheromones 17
philosophy 244
phone calls 202, 203, 338, 352
physical affection 64, 328, 344, 412
physical reactions 17, 20
pickiness 160, 162
picture, love as 16
playfulness 236

playing around 278
pleasures 180
pointlessness, marriage 375
political views 156
porn, soft 86
positivity 53, 302, 399, 406, 426
possessiveness 15, 417
practical teamwork 33
praise 77
pre-nuptial agreements 273
pregnancy 360–1
present, living in 249
pride 253
priorities 342, 370
private reflection 197
problems
    dealing with 404
    relationships 140, 201
    sex 314, 320
    sharing 73, 171
    solving 54, 55, 141, 143, 178, 215
    stress 236
    talking 211
    trust 300
promises 288, 291–3
promoting love when apart 262

promotions, work 369
protecting love 228, 233
psychological reactions 17, 20
public, behaviour in 161, 190
put downs 194

Quarrels *see* arguments
questions 109, 199
quickie sex 310, 311, 323
quiet, going *see* silence
quiet time 197

Reading 329
real self
    change 418
    eccentricity 22
    inhibiting 350
    mid-life 375
    shyness 49, 286
    supportiveness 243
    work-life balance 370
rebuilding love 395
reconciliation 427
reconnection 200
redundancy 66
relationships
    addressing issues 171
    books on 176
    changing gear 110
    complex 249
    definitions of loving
    relationships 224
    doubts 70
    effect on others 21
    end of 347
    exploring 229
    failing 168
    fear 61, 62, 175, 247
    good 344, 345, 399
    great 172
    as living thing 13
    maintaining 181
    making changes in 74
    making it work 172–81, 393
    priority 219
    problems 140
    putting into 237
    relaxing in 176
    rescuing 401–19
    revitalizing 377
    troubled 157–71
    uniqueness 227
    see also living together;
marriage
relaxation 176, 264
reliability 278, 292, 413

religions 36
replaying arguments 256, 259
requests 207
resentments 21
respect 16, 155, 194, 277
responsibility 401
retirement 380, 382–4
riches *see* wealth
rings 128, 130
roller-coaster, love as 256
romance 27, 96–9, 239–41
room, own 33
rough touch 194
rough words 416
rows *see* arguments
rudeness 169, 194, 416
rules of love 343

Sarcasm 142, 194, 403, 404
scent 32
self *see* identity; real self
self-approval 60
self-confidence 52–5, 71,
    80–9, 189, 245
    see also confidence
self-depreciating talk 113
self-esteem 48, 56–79, 298
self-love 48–51, 272

self-respect 294
self-sabotaging 113
self-sacrifice 13
selfishness 50, 180
senses 330
sensuality 330–9
separate lives 170
separation 392, 394, 396, 397
sex
  affection 64
  athletic 30
  attitudes to 310–14
  avoiding 82
  books on 325
  boredom 324, 325
  brains 316
  casual 306
  confidence 88
  desire 18–19, 27, 318–20
  dynamic of 31
  enjoying 29, 81
  ex-partners 426
  experience 315
  fantasies 85
  feeling used 81, 310
  frequency 82, 85, 86,
    312–13, 326, 328
  good 30, 320
  'good in bed' 31

holidays 309
initiating 86
joy of 306–8
light on during 335
and love 306, 344
men 310, 324
mid-life 379
with others 133
places for 338
problems 314, 320
process of 316–17
quickie 310, 311, 323
refusing 327
regenerating 405
romance 27, 28
routine 88
self-confidence 80–9
silence 220
size 315
spiritual 37
splitting up 391
stopping 366
talking 219–21, 336–8
technique 322–6
time for 323
trust 426
on TV 80
unwelcome demands 402
videos 325

and wellbeing 306–39
sex drive 82, 310, 312, 321,
    327–9
sex therapists 87
sexiness 30
sexuality 28, 307
shaky patches 247–56,
    258–60
sharing, thoughts 22, 202
sharing a home
    see living together
shopping 34, 158
shouting 166, 186, 198, 230
showing love 246, 398
shyness 49, 107, 151, 377
silence 174, 205, 212, 215,
    220
simple pleasures 180
single people 12, 235
size, sexual matters 315
sky at night 239
sleep 245, 260, 264, 334
smiling 263, 336
smoking 138
social life 26, 53
soft porn 86
solutions 141, 215
sorrow 11, 384
sorry, saying see apologizing

soul mates 40, 41, 43
space to think 395
spiritual beliefs 36–9, 155
splitting up, sex 391
spontaneity 116, 172, 207, 234
spring 94
stress 236, 319, 372
successes 67
sudoku 25
sulking 215, 251
supportiveness 67, 243–6, 261–5, 273
suspicion 272, 413
swimming 24

Table manners 109
talking 208–16
  art of 214
  best time for 186
  blessing of 187
  clarity 198
  closeness 101
  dangers of 191, 194
  harsh 142, 198
  healing 201
  'I love you' 202, 291
  importance of 200
  and listening 214, 253
  love 190
  lovingly 184
  mean 158
  negative 186
  not talking 196, 197, 225
  positive 195
  practise 185
  problems 211
  questions 199
  rough 416
  self-depreciating 113
  sex 219–21, 336–8
  special way 195
  subjects 204
  taking turns 216
  time together 204, 217
  timing of 208, 209
  tiredness 209, 210
  see also words
tangrams 25
tasks 136, 168
  see also chores
team-work 152
teasing 354
teenage love 347–8
television 80, 414–15
tension 145
texting 353

therapy 314, 420–2
thoughts
  challenging 242
  honesty 253
  loving 19
  self-esteem 50
  sexual 316, 317
  sharing 22, 202
  space to think 395
time, management of 355
time apart 79, 236, 264, 365,
    392
time together
  amount 77, 235
  eating 367
  enjoying 144, 145
  going out 77, 404, 414
  listening 209
  making 79, 178, 179,
    217–19, 411
  talking 204, 217
timidity 53
tiredness 29, 80, 178, 209,
    210, 319
touch 241, 330, 331–5
touchiness 414
trapped, feeling 379
treasuring love 231
trial separation 392, 394

troubled relationships 157–71
true love 12, 249
true self see real self
trust 268–303
  courage to 270
  definition 268
  developing 181
  distrust of 284
  importance of 275
  inspiring 268–83
  rebuilding 300–3
  self-esteem 75, 124
  sex 426
  trusting in 296–9
  in yourself 269
trustworthiness 276, 280, 281,
    293
truth 103, 285
turning towards partner 263,
    319
TV 80, 414–15

Unconditional love 12
understanding 153, 164,
    184–92, 194–207
unfaithfulness see affairs
unhappiness 158
uniqueness 227

see also individuality
unkindness 65, 194, 228, 250, 393
upsets, unintentional 196

Valentine's Day 99
vibrancy, early love 394
vicious talk 198
videos 325
voice 94, 103, 202, 337
voluntary work 100, 378
vulnerability 72

Warmth 174
weaknesses, guarding against 274
wealth i96, 123, 355
wedding rings 128
weddings 38, 127
wit 404
women 310, 311, 312, 381, 382
wonder, sense of 239
words 72, 205, 206, 207, 213
    see also talking
work 78, 100, 218, 368
    see also careers

work-life balance 365–71
worrying 54, 254
writing 423

notes

notes

notes

notes